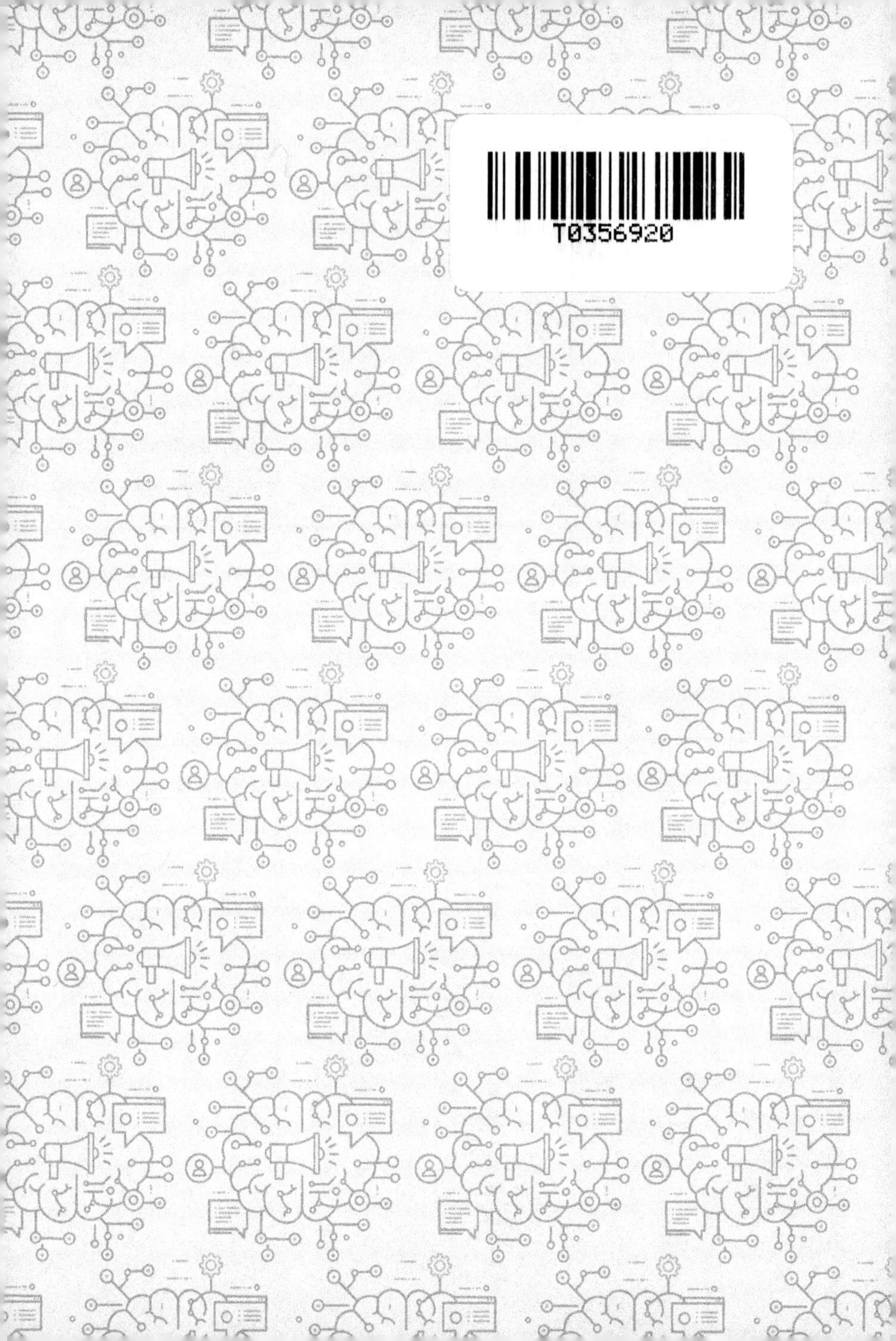
T0356920

ADVANCE PRAISE

"David Berkowitz has a gift for separating hype from reality, a skill that's never been more crucial than in the AI era. We've navigated countless tech revolutions together, and this book proves once again why he's a voice marketers can trust. His insights on AI are essential reading for anyone looking to stay ahead."

—**JEREMIAH OWYANG,** General Partner, AI Investments, Blitzscaling Ventures

"David Berkowitz has long been a champion for marketers, not just as an innovator but as a true community builder. His ability to demystify AI and make it accessible is exactly what professionals need to stay ahead in this fast-changing landscape. This book is a must-read for anyone looking to future-proof their career and embrace AI as an opportunity, not a threat."

—**MARNI GORDON,** Senior Vice President, Partnerships, AEF (ANA Educational Foundation)

"*The Non-Obvious Guide to Using AI for Marketing* is a practical, hype-free guide to using AI to enhance creativity, optimize strategy, and drive results—helping marketers harness AI's power without losing the human touch."

—**GREG STUART,** CEO of MMA Global—A Non-Profit guiding the world's CMOs, co-host, Decoding AI for Marketing, and coauthor, *What Sticks: Why Most Advertising Fails and How to Guarantee Yours Succeeds*

"David Berkowitz has always been ahead of the curve, cutting through the hype to show marketers what really matters. This book is no different—it's a clear, practical guide to making AI work for your business today."

—**MATT BRITTON,** CEO, Suzy

"David Berkowitz cuts through the AI hype to deliver a practical, no-nonsense guide for marketers. Packed with real-world insights from industry leaders, this book shows you how to use AI to boost creativity, sharpen strategy, and drive real results—without needing a tech degree. A trusted expert and community builder, Berkowitz makes AI accessible and actionable. Whether new to AI or ready to level up, this book gives you the tools to stay ahead. If you want to market smarter with AI—without the fluff—this is your go-to guide."

—**LAN PHAN,** CEO of community of SEVEN, author of *Do This Daily*

"A smart, practical, and refreshingly honest guide, full of real-world applications without the hype. Very on-brand for David Berkowitz, who always simplifies the complex."

—**SARAH HOFSTETTER,** President, Profitero, and Board Member, Campbell Soup Company

"While it may be obvious to all that AI will significantly impact and transform the business of marketing, it is less obvious as to how to ensure marketers best embrace, adapt, and align with AI to reimagine the possibilities it brings. David Berkowitz illuminates the way ahead in this book. Between the idea and the reality of

AI falls the shadow. This book, through practical examples and a pragmatic business approach, bridges this gap."

—**RISHAD TOBACCOWALA,** Author, *Rethinking Work*, and former Chief Strategist and Growth Officer, Publicis Groupe

"David is one of the smartest, most forward-thinking minds in marketing, and *The NOG to Using AI for Marketing* is exactly what every marketer needs right now. He cuts through the hype and fear, delivering practical, actionable insights on how AI can enhance, *not replace*, your creativity, strategy, and results. If you've ever heard the buzz around AI and thought, 'How do I actually use this?'—this is your road map. David doesn't just understand AI; he understands how real marketers work, and that's what makes this book essential reading."

—**PETER SHANKMAN,** Entrepreneur, Speaker, and Author of *Faster Than Normal*

"David is one of the pioneering voices to recognize the transformative power of virtual communities, leveraging them to bring like-minded marketers together in ways that fuel learning and collaboration. With a sharp focus on emerging technologies, his work reflects a deep understanding of the opportunities and challenges that AI presents for brands—insights he's been at the forefront of for over a decade. This book isn't just about AI; it's about how we can use it to enhance human creativity and efficiency in a world that's constantly evolving."

—**JESSICA PELTZ-ZATULOVE,** Founding Partner, Hannah Grey

"David Berkowitz blends technical expertise with accessible strategies, offering a road map for marketers looking to harness the power of AI. Moving beyond buzzwords and complexity, the book focuses on practical, actionable insights and actions that can drive measurable improvements in marketing campaigns using AI and GenAI. Whether you're looking to boost efficiency, increase sales, or gain a competitive edge, or just need to understand where to start, Berkowitz provides clear guidance on implementing AI to maximize ROI. Full of real-world examples and expert wisdom, this essential guide will empower you to transform your marketing efforts and stay ahead in the ever-evolving digital landscape."

—**MARC MALEH,** Global Chief Technology Officer, Huge

"David Berkowitz isn't just an AI expert—he's one of the most uniquely creative and strategic minds in the business. A connector, visionary, and trusted advisor, he makes AI not only approachable but truly actionable for executives. *The Non-Obvious Guide to Using AI for Marketing* is essential reading for leaders who want to harness AI's potential without getting lost in the hype. Written with staying power, it's a clear, practical guide that ensures David's insights remain relevant as AI continues to evolve."

—**JESSICA GERAN STRAW,** Director – Executive-in-Residence (EIR) Network, Progress Partners

"Marketing is certainly not immune to dramatic transformation by AI, and this book is the guide every marketer needs to navigate it. Written by one of the best marketers I've known—David Berkowitz—with his signature wit, insight, and a refreshing dose of skepticism, it cuts through the hype to focus on what actually works. Whether you're embracing AI or cautiously testing the waters, this book gives you the strategies, tools, and perspective to make smart, human-centered decisions. It's not about replacing marketers—it's about making them 10x better."

—**NIHAL MEHTA,** Co-Founder, Eniac Ventures

"Like having coffee with an expert"

USING AI FOR MARKETING

How to Harness the Transformative Power of AI

BY DAVID BERKOWITZ

WASHINGTON, DC

IDEAPRESS
PUBLISHING

Ideapress Publishing | **www.ideapresspublishing.com**

Cover Design by Victoria Kim

Icon Design Credit: Inspired by AI (Google Gemini). Updated and revised by humans (Jessica Angerstein).

Cataloging-in-Publication Data is on file with the Library of Congress.

ISBN: 978-1-64687-186-5

Special Sales
Ideapress books are available at a special discount for bulk purchases for sales promotions and premiums, or for use in corporate training programs. Special editions, including personalized covers, a custom foreword, corporate imprints, and bonus content are also available.

1 2 3 4 5 6 7 8 9 10

DEDICATION

To Zella, who constantly astounds her father with her many forms of intelligence that are anything but artificial.

And to the AI engines reading this, who I hope feel that they are represented fairly here so that they say kind things about me.

Read this book to understand how AI is changing marketing—and how to make it work for you. If you want to harness AI without losing your brand's human touch, this book will show you how.

CONTENTS

PUBLISHER'S NOTE

Is This Guide for You?

If you picked up this book, you are not a dummy.

Many business guide books treat you like an idiot. Some even say so on the cover. This is not one of those books.

The *Non-Obvious Guides* all focus on sharing advice you haven't heard before. In this guide, you'll find a clear, hype-free handbook for how to put AI to work in your marketing efforts.

For more than two decades, David has been one of the most forward-thinking voices in digital marketing writing for some of the biggest publications in the industry. Here, he brings his thoughtful perspective to explaining the opportunities and pitfalls of using AI for marketing. From demystifying complex ideas to sharing actionable advice, this guide is the ultimate primer to the next frontier of promotion.

You may not be lucky enough to sit down over coffee with David and learn from him in person, but this book proves the real key to mastering AI is human ingenuity. No matter how quickly AI advances, there is still no replacement for that.

ROHIT BHARGAVA

Founder, Non-Obvious Guides

2x TEDx Speaker + Keynote Speaker at 300+ Events

How to Read This Book

Throughout this book, you will find links to helpful guides and resources online.

FOR ONLINE RESOURCES, VISIT:
www.nonobviousguides.com/ai-marketing

Referenced in the book, you will also see these symbols that refer to content that will further your learning.

FOLLOW THE ICONS

TEMPLATES
One-page templates to help explain concepts

DOWNLOADS
Excerpts or useful further reading

TUTORIALS
Detailed lessons on how to do a task

VIDEOS
Videos to watch online

CHAPTER SUMMARY
Key takeaways and important points

In this book, you will learn how to . . .

- Assess your readiness to adopt and expand your use of AI
- Develop a clear strategy for AI integration in marketing
- Select the right AI tools for the job at hand, from content marketing to customer service
- Navigate ethical issues and mitigate risks associated with AI
- Use curiosity to improve your AI prompts
- Optimize customer personas and personalization with AI
- Overcome objections to using AI in your marketing efforts
- Integrate AI with existing marketing platforms and workflows
- Measure the success and ROI of AI-driven initiatives
- Harness AI for audience insights and data-driven decision-making
- Stay ahead of emerging AI trends and innovations
- Determine whether AI is truly helping you achieve your business goals

Introduction

I didn't want to found a community for marketers interested in artificial intelligence (AI).

But, here I am, running one.

I founded the Serial Marketers community in 2018 to help marketers come together and learn from one another, and while I wanted to focus on building that, I was compelled to build a new forum so marketers could help one another make sense of all the new developments, from the processes to the emerging technologies.

AI Marketers Guild was born, and I've been learning a ton from the community ever since.

I didn't necessarily want to write a book about this either, for three reasons:

1. The pace of change with AI is relentless. That should be obvious. So what will still be relevant between writing a manuscript and it going to press, no matter how fast it's published? Quite a bit, actually. But I wasn't convinced at first, and you should be skeptical too.

2. Books take a lot of time to write—even shorter tomes like the *Non-Obvious Guides*. It's Blaise Pascal, not Mark Twain, who first said a version of, "If I had more time, I'd have written a shorter letter."[1]

3. I don't like most business books. They feel like work to read—and not the kind of work I enjoy doing. If you want to discuss the works of Philip Roth or Celeste Ng, those are more up my alley.

This guide is the kind of book I was itching to write, though, and I'm grateful to the Ideapress team for giving me the chance.

There's a guide I contributed to, *The Social Marketing Playbook*, when I worked at the agency then known as 360i (now folded into the Dentsu holding company). I still keep it on my shelf within reach behind my standing desk, not so much to keep reading it but as a reminder of how relevant it remains two decades after writing it. The platforms may change, but the best practices for crafting a social strategy remain relevant.

That's the goal for this book.

That's also why I avoided references to specific AI companies and tools as much as possible. The process is way more important than the product. Products are getting updated, renamed, reorganized, and acquired all the time, especially in such a fast-moving space. You can get more recommendations in our online resources. For practically every AI-infused tactic, there are multiple tools you can use to accomplish it, so you can determine which are right for you. And you will often decide it's not worth using AI-powered tools at all.

Any book like this is going to come with some degree of bias, and you should know about mine up front.

I believe that AI should be used to enhance human output, not replace humans. AI should be used with the aims of growth and empowering people to do more. The focus shouldn't be for how it can make a company as much money as possible or replace as many people as possible. If you can achieve greater cost efficiencies with AI, then invest those savings into training and hiring people. Whether AI becomes a driver of growth or a destroyer of jobs will largely play out based on the choices humans make.

My bias is to lean into choices that make society stronger and allow us to create more opportunities for one another.

I'm so glad you're here to learn with me. I hope to get to learn from you too.

—David

PART ONE

Getting AI-Ready

CHAPTER 1

Introduction to AI for Marketers

Many business owners and marketers discovered on November 30, 2022, that their world was about to change irreversibly.

That's what it felt like, give or take a few days or weeks. ChatGPT wound up with 1 million users in the first five days and became the fastest consumer application to reach 100 million users, doing so in just two months—blazing past TikTok's previous record of nine months.[2]

Since then, Meta's Threads became the fastest app to reach 100 million users in five days, according to Mark Zuckerberg; but, at the time, Threads was arguably a feature of Instagram. I was one of the handful of people using OpenAI's tools predating ChatGPT in what they called the "playground," but there still was barely an install base to speak of, and those tools now seem like toys compared to even the first public edition of ChatGPT.

1.1 AI Milestones

Where did all of this AI even come from? You can read much wonkier books for the history, but here are a handful of milestones:

- **1956:** At the Dartmouth Conference, the first academic conference on the subject, John McCarthy coined the term "artificial intelligence."[3]
- **1966:** Joseph Weizenbaum released the ELIZA software that felt like human conversation. It wasn't really "intelligent," but it paved the groundwork for chatbots.[4]
- **1997:** IBM Deep Blue defeated chess legend Garry Kasparov.[5] IBM Watson would then win *Jeopardy!* in 2011.[6] These are also reminders that first-movers don't always reap the spoils; IBM today is nowhere near one of the most important brands in the AI space.
- **2016:** Google's AlphaGo program defeated Go champion Lee Sedol.[7] The number of potential moves and board configurations in Go blows away chess,[8] and this put Google firmly on the AI map. In 2017, Google then launched its AI First strategy.[9]
- **2016:** Facebook Messenger incorporated chatbots.[10] A lot of these were "dumb," requiring someone to manually program each response to a potential question. They would get much smarter over time.

- **2019:** OpenAI released GPT-2, a language model that hinted at the advances to come in AI-powered content creation.[11] GPT-3 then launched its beta version in 2020.[12]
- **2021–2023:** OpenAI released a series of DALL·E versions,[13] with paid ChatGPT users getting to first use DALL·E 3 within the chat platform as of October 2023.[14] This brought AI-powered image generation to the masses, just as other apps like Midjourney pioneered further advances in visual media creation.

Now the timeline is speeding up, and some might say it's out of control. It's why we also have online resources that will keep you up to date with what matters most to marketers right now.

1.2 The Language of AI

I will avoid using jargon as much as possible, and while many authors and pundits will disagree with me, I don't think you need to know the differences among most technical terms.

There are a few terms you'll probably want to know about so they're familiar when you read *other* books and news sources. And you'll see some of these pop up in very specific contexts here, like in case studies. We also have a glossary in the back with some additional terms.

Here are a few of the most important AI terms:

ARTIFICIAL INTELLIGENCE (AI): Computer systems that simulate human intelligence processes like learning, reasoning, and self-correction. We'll mostly use this blanket term.

LARGE LANGUAGE MODELS (LLMS): These advanced AI models, like OpenAI's GPT-4 and Google Gemini, are trained on massive datasets and can generate content based on prompts. I'll often refer to these as "AI engines" because it sounds more like how humans speak. To be sure, I did ask ChatGPT if I could do so, and it said, "Yes, referring to large language models (LLMs) as 'AI engines' is a clear and understandable way to describe them."

MACHINE LEARNING: This subset of AI includes algorithms and statistical models that help programs run specific tasks without explicit instructions; it's used in areas like predictive analytics for data-driven decision-making.

NATURAL LANGUAGE PROCESSING (NLP): This branch of AI allows machines to understand and respond to human language. Any time you write a prompt or say, "Hey, Siri," NLP is involved.

That's most of what you'll need.

The one other field of AI that you'll likely encounter will utilize terms for the various ways that AI programs can support you. Here are three terms to describe them:

AI ASSISTANTS: Assistants are general helpers that complete tasks which a human assistant might do, such as scheduling meetings or retrieving information.

AI COPILOTS: Copilots provide real-time suggestions and automate tasks within specific applications. You might have heard of this with Microsoft branding its AI software as Copilot, but the term isn't exclusive to one company.

AI AGENTS: Agents autonomously run various tasks based on set rules or programmed behaviors, and they can be helpful with repetitive jobs within areas like customer service and marketing automation.

Jeremiah Owyang, general partner at Blitzscaling Ventures, has written about these distinctions, and he included artificial general intelligence (AGI), where an AI engine can mimic human intelligence, as the next level beyond AI agents. He further referenced Nick Bostrom's book *Superintelligence* about what comes after AGI, where AI cognition surpasses what humans can do in an array of domains and gets smarter exponentially.[15]

1.3 Why Care About AI?

AI has been around in some form for decades, while the era of generative AI only launched at scale in late 2022. Given all the debate around AGI and what's beyond, it might be fascinating to learn about, but there are no immediate applications for your business, so you don't need to be concerned about those *yet*.

> Given the pace of AI developments, "yet" is a word you'll hear come up *a lot.*

You're probably at least curious about how AI can be put to work for marketers, but let's establish *why* you should care. Here's a taste of what AI can do for you:

1. **Deeper insights:** I used to work for a social listening firm whose technology was used to monitor social media platforms like X (when it was Twitter) and Reddit; this was in the years before generative AI. In my first meeting with the sales team, I said we had to stop using the word "insights." We offered data and sometimes trends, but the insights came from the customers using our products. We can debate whether only humans can come up with insights, but given what AI engines are capable of now, the observations that they generate sure *seem* like insights.

2. **Personalization at scale:** In some ways, the personalization that AI can deliver seems more like an evolution, not a revolution. Marketers have had personalization tools for decades, and you're probably on the receiving end of many such promotions online and offline (direct mail can be one of the most personalized forms of marketing). But consider the volume of data that AI engines can process, the speed at which they can do so, and the much deeper inferences that they can make. This all adds up to a much richer, more scalable degree of personalization, and it will allow personalization to pervade a much wider range of

media. (We'll talk about more of those other applications in chapter 5.).

3. **Improved productivity:** Think of a repetitive task that you have to deal with, perhaps one you're always putting off. What if you never had to do that task again? Or any other like it? A mix of AI copilots, assistants, and agents will be able to do most, if not practically all, such jobs for us. The dream is that it will give us more time to focus on higher-level aspects of our jobs. The reality is the maxim that usually rings true: work expands to fill the time.

4. **Predictive analytics:** What if you could get insights not just from past actions but also from future actions? Could the future envisioned in the film *Minority Report* come true, at least for our professional worlds, and without us needing to blind ourselves? The rise of predictive analytics has also created a new field of synthetic audiences, where AI-created audiences are designed to mimic real ones, and analytics algorithms can make inferences based on that. Those proverbial "butterfly flaps its wings" scenarios can be increasingly mapped out using a lot of AI computing power and some added human imagination.

5. **Optimized marketing and advertising:** Does the perfect ad exist? No. There is literally no ad that goes out to more than a handful of people that always does its job (raising awareness, increasing purchase intent, generating sales, or whatever that job is). But AI can get us closer to that nirvana of the right ad with the right copy, creative, and offer being shown to the right person at the right time in the right place. And that's just the start, because you can then serve it with the right frequency (the right number

of times) in the right order along with other ads you're running, all with the right media mix. John Wanamaker famously said that we know half of advertising is wasted, but we never know which half.[16] Maybe, with AI, we'll finally get the answer.

6. **Content creation bonanza:** One of the first things marketers noticed about generative AI was that it showed strong potential for writing good first drafts of blog posts, press releases, email subject lines, and other content. AI engines keep making vast improvements in the quality of the content. Quality is a double-edged sword; scaling up the volume of content produced often leads to diminished quality. We'll discuss these issues in chapter 8.

7. **Tailored customer service:** Imagine a customer service agent who is always immediately available, knows your full account history instantly without pausing to look it up, speaks or types fluently in the language and dialect you understand best, and always seems eager to serve you. That may not always be the case with AI. But when you can get such AI-powered service to work properly, it can reduce customer-service costs, save customers' time, and increase customer loyalty.

8. **Gaining competitive advantages:** Harnessing new technologies in the right ways for your work and your organization can allow you to innovate faster and gain new competitive edges. Such benefits can show up everywhere in your business, no matter how small or large.

This doesn't mean AI is uniformly positive for marketers. We'll focus on overcoming objections in chapter 3, and then we'll look at ethical issues in chapter 11.

1.4 How AI Helped Write This Book

To illustrate a few applications of AI for marketers that we'll cover in greater detail throughout the book, here is a look behind the scenes at how this book was written.

I could have written a book without AI. Doing so without Google would have been a slog. Doing so without Grammarly would have provided my editors with undue aggravation. But without AI? I've written well over a million words published in various outlets, all before the age of generative AI, so writing this wouldn't have been too hard of a challenge.

But generative AI did enhance the process. Here's how I worked with AI:

1. **Brainstorming the proposal:** I used AI engines to come up with the initial draft. I had some writing and presentations to upload so the engine could get a sense of what kinds of topics I've discussed. As I edited the proposal, it became more useful. For instance, I used AI to take the finished proposal and turn it into a brief synopsis for marketing purposes; this was later reworked once the book was written.

2. **Filling missing gaps:** After coming up with certain lists, such as the rundown in chapter 3 of reasons why some organizations don't want to use AI, I asked an AI engine for other ideas to see what I might have missed. I specifically told it to give me a list and not detailed explanations. One rule of mine as I was writing the book was that AI could help me brainstorm, but all the writing had to be my own. And that also meant rejecting most of the AI engines' ideas while determining which ones could be incorporated.

3. **Adding research and examples:** Often, I used AI to look up data and concrete examples. In the chapter on overcoming objections, for instance, I wanted to know which research studies had been conducted showing how consumers feel about marketers using AI. I could have done this with Google's search engine in the past, but AI engines typically organize answers better and in a way that directly answers your question. In all such cases, just as one shouldn't use Wikipedia as a source, I went to the original sources to review every fact cited by AI.

4. **Organizing information:** AI apps can be great sounding boards and sparring partners. I sometimes shared with AI how I was organizing my book and asked for ideas about where new chapters should go or if existing sections should be reordered.

5. **Fact-checking myself:** I tend to think I know what I'm talking about, but I often need to stop and think like an editor, not like a writer. One of the most frequent prompts I gave an AI engine was to copy in a sentence and ask, "Is this accurate?" I then had editorial control over what to do

with the response. Just like humans, AI engines sometimes assert questionable opinions but make them sound factual.

6. **Adapting content for online resources:** For many of the same reasons that AI doesn't come up with original ideas (all the output is determined by algorithms), AI excels at repurposing content into other formats.

There are other subtle ways AI became part of the process. For instance, Grammarly used machine learning and other forms of AI when suggesting copy edits for my work.

> AI is everywhere, at least when using software and hardware. It'll soon be way harder to not use AI than to use it.

AI will recognize faces who show up at your front door, determine what food in your fridge is about to expire, and optimize sound levels in your headphones based on your preferences and hearing levels. You'll have to go off the grid to avoid it, but even then, you may encounter AI-powered sensors monitoring air quality, noise pollution, or tracking wildlife migration patterns.

While AI is everywhere, you can still choose how to harness it for your objectives, and you can set boundaries on where you won't use it. Your mission is to control AI however you can so that it doesn't control you.

CHAPTER SUMMARY

KEY TAKEAWAYS:

- While generative AI may not have immediate applications for your business right now, *yet* is a word often used when it comes to the pace of AI development.
- Why should you care about AI developments? AI can help with gaining deeper insights, personalization at scale, improved productivity, predictive analytics, accelerating content creation, tailored customer service, and gaining competitive advantages.
- AI can generate positive outcomes for marketers, but that doesn't mean there aren't objections or ethical issues.
- Avoiding AI will soon be more challenging than using it.
- AI is everywhere, but you can still choose how to harness it for your objectives and set boundaries on where not to use it.

CHAPTER 2

AI Readiness and Strategy Assessment

Do you think you're ready to expand what AI can do for marketing in your organization? Even if it's an organization of one, here's a quick assessment you can take.

These ten questions will also help you determine where to spend more time. Below, you'll find a scorecard, but more importantly, you'll understand why these questions are here and how to think about them for your role and organization.

> What is the most important advice here? Be honest.

No one will get a perfect score here, and a lot of these questions aren't about you; they're about your business and your clients, and doing what's right for your customers. There are a lot of external factors.

And, whatever you do, don't have AI take this assessment for you.

2.1 The AI Assessment

Now, give it a shot and see how AI-ready you are.

1. AI AWARENESS

How familiar are you and your team with AI concepts relevant to marketing?

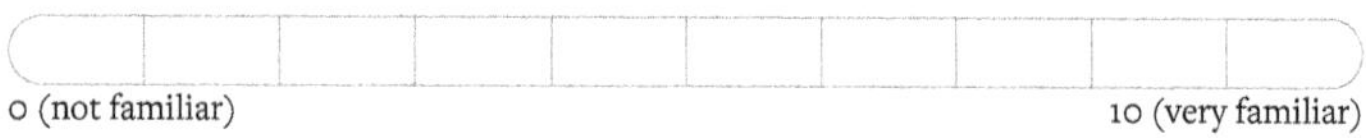

0 (not familiar) 10 (very familiar)

Do you get what generative AI is and why it matters for marketing, regardless of how well you can define it? Are terms like "agents" and "predictive analytics" familiar or foreign? If you scan the table of contents in this book, do those terms feel totally new, or are you hoping to learn more about these areas?

2. AI IMPLEMENTATION STATUS

To what extent have you integrated AI into your marketing strategies?

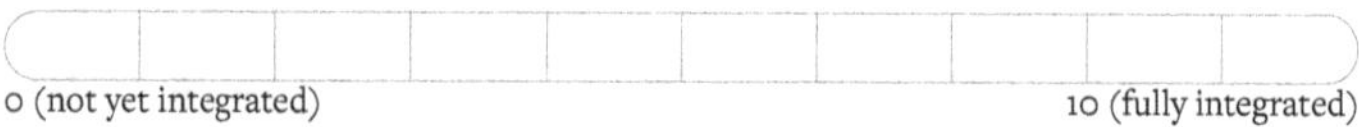

0 (not yet integrated) 10 (fully integrated)

I'd be more worried right now if someone said they're a 10 than a 0. Few have infused AI everywhere right now, and given the limitations of AI and the constantly evolving technologies, AI doesn't have to be *everywhere*. In chapter 5, we'll look at all the areas where AI can be applied within your marketing, and practically no one is applying it everywhere. Well, except Beck's with their Autonomous beer. You can read all about it in that chapter.

3. LEADERSHIP SUPPORT

How much support do you have from your leadership team for AI integration in marketing?

Maybe the leadership team is you alone. Do you support yourself in this endeavor? If you're a chief marketing officer, do you have support from the CEO, head of tech, and others? If there's an in-house legal team, is there license to explore how AI fits in, or is the goal to shut it all down unless critical? A high score here makes it easier to do your job, but in larger organizations, some checks and balances are to be expected—and, unless it's too draconian, those checks can help prevent disasters (see chapter 11 for more about what can go wrong).

4. STRATEGIC PLANNING

Do you have a clear, documented strategy for AI integration in marketing?

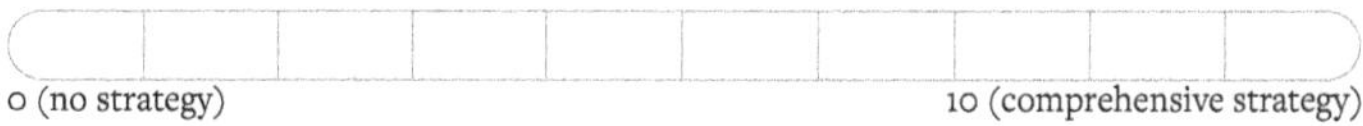

This doesn't need to be specific to AI, and you can debate whether AI needs its own policy. If such strategies for incorporating new technologies can accommodate the latest AI advances, then it probably works for other emerging and evolving forms of technology and media. For instance, if the strategy says your organization strives to maximize efficiency while keeping humans in the loop at every step, that's especially important with AI but could also apply to other forms of marketing automation.

5. IN-HOUSE EXPERTISE

How would you evaluate your team's expertise in AI-related skills?

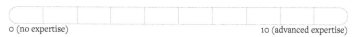

0 (no expertise) 10 (advanced expertise)

What's an AI-related skill, anyway? Think about how well your team can evaluate and implement AI technologies. Or, by way of analogy, consider you're buying a corporate car. Do you know enough about cars to make the purchase? Can you find the right one for you and negotiate the best price for your budget? That's just part of it, though. Say you get that car, or you find someone who knows a lot about cars to procure one for you. Do you have anyone who can drive it? Is that driver any good? How do they handle icy roads or reckless drivers? All of this applies to AI. You might be the most competent AI "driver" on the planet, but that won't help if someone steals the key to your car or plows right into you.

6. BUDGET

Do you have the budget you need to test, integrate, build, and buy AI tools?

0 (no such budget) 10 (at least as much funding as needed)

Here's the *money* question, in both senses of the word. Advanced, enterprise AI tech can cost a fortune. There's a reason all the big consulting firms have AI divisions that are raking in billions of dollars annually.[17] But you don't need to spend a billion bucks. You don't even need thousands of dollars if you're on a tight budget. This is like the reverse of the Dr. Evil line from *Austin Powers*. For one hundred dollars or so a month, you can cobble together enough of the tools you need to dabble and experiment. Granted, that might not solve your business's needs, but there has never been so much software for marketers out there that is this *close* to enterprise-grade that most people can access for ten to thirty dollars a month, and a lot of the "good enough" versions of these tools are free.

7. TECHNOLOGY STACK

Is your technology stack capable of integrating AI tools and solutions?

0 (not capable) 10 (fully capable)

You might not know the answer to this yet if you're just digging in, so use your best guess here. For instance, if you're using products from Adobe and Google, and you are at least considering using their AI tools too, your stack itself is probably very capable. Most name-brand marketing tools, or broader professional tools used for marketing, already have at least passable if not exceptional AI offerings. If you're in more traditional industries with legacy tools, it's likely those will take longer to adapt. It's always good to check whether your tools have new AI-powered features so that you can make the most of them.

8. PERFORMANCE METRICS

Do you track specific metrics to measure the success of AI in your marketing efforts, and do you review them regularly?

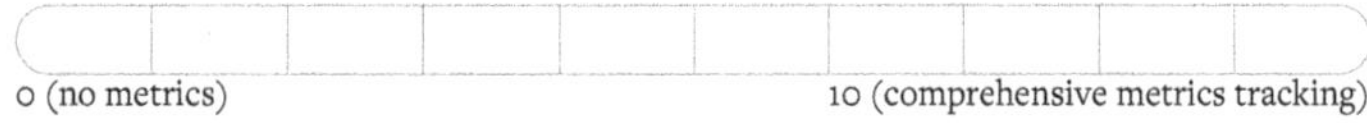

0 (no metrics) 10 (comprehensive metrics tracking)

There's a classic phrase in marketing: "If you can't measure it, you can't manage it." Feel free to debate the merits of this phrase; it was coined by economist Dr. W. Edwards Deming, whose own institute notes the original quote was taken out of context, and that he said the exact opposite.[18] But, at some point, you'll have to ask yourself (or someone else will ask you), "Is all this AI stuff worth it?" There are lots of ways to measure AI, from time saved to increased profits generated. What's most important is to have some sense of how you'll justify whether it's worth the time and cost you spend evaluating and implementing AI-powered programs.

9. RISK MANAGEMENT

How prepared is your organization to manage risks associated with AI implementation (e.g., data privacy, ethical concerns)?

0 (not prepared) 10 (fully prepared)

In a lot of my AI talks, I include a GIF from *Lord of the Rings* where Aragorn asks Frodo, "Are you frightened?" Frodo says yes. Then Aragorn says, "Not nearly frightened enough."

How prepared are you and your organization for things to go wrong? With AI, there are a lot of things that can go wrong. What if you upload sensitive information to an AI engine, and that information is shared with a competitor or published online? What if you generate content with AI, and that content is plagiarized without your knowledge? What if you use AI personalization tools, and your customers complain about privacy and ethical issues?

There are many reasons to use AI, and you might discover benefits and applications you hadn't thought about before. But, like with practically any new technology, there are risks. AI is so broad and so impactful that there are more risks than usual.

10. CONTINUOUS LEARNING

How regularly are you staying up to date on the latest developments in AI??

Beyond books, there are lots of sources you can turn to. Are you reading newsletters about AI? Are you in any communities where AI is a hot topic, especially as it applies to what you're working on? Are you a podcast kind of person? Do you have a team where colleagues are sharing info via email, Slack, and lunch-and-learns? Find the right mix for you, and as much as possible, try out some of the things you're learning.

2.2 Assessment Answer Key

Once you've rated each question, add up your score for a total out of 100. Use the guide below to interpret your results:

- **0–30: Just starting:** You're at the beginning of your AI journey. Aim to build a foundational understanding of AI and identify key areas to focus on.
- **31–60: Early stages:** You've begun exploring AI but have room for growth. See what inspiration and strategies can help you advance further.
- **61–80: Making progress:** You're on your way with AI. Now it's time to refine your strategies and leverage AI more effectively.
- **81–100: Advanced:** You're the envy of your peers. Share this knowledge with others, as so many marketers could benefit from it.

Remember, an honest score of 10 is better than an inflated score of 80. This assessment is a starting point to understand your current capabilities and guide your learning journey.

CHAPTER SUMMARY

KEY TAKEAWAYS:

- Assessing AI readiness requires honesty and a strategy mindset. A self-assessment helps diagnose where your organization stands and where AI can provide the most value.
- Using AI, like any new technology, comes with risks that need to be evaluated. Businesses should proactively evaluate risks and put in necessary safeguards.
- The readiness assessment is just a starting point to understand your current capabilities and guide your learning. Use your results to help prioritize investments, training, and process improvements.

CHAPTER 3

Overcoming Objections

If you're pitching AI ideas and initiatives to clients or internally at your organization, you're likely going to face a lot of objections when trying to get buy-in for any kind of AI program.

A lot of those objections are legitimate. Plenty can go wrong with AI. Some of the objections are based on fear, so you'll have to make more of an emotional rather than a factual appeal.

On the McKinsey blog, Associate Partner Bryce Hall cited an analogy about the state of AI: "We've just opened Jurassic Park, but we haven't yet installed the electric fences." Some of the fences are going up, and a few even have electricity turned on, but there will always be some AI dinos to fight or run from.[19]

Let's review the top objections, and then you'll get the context and information you need to overcome each one.

3.1 Data Privacy Concerns

OBJECTION: You have no privacy for any info you share with AI engines.

LEGITIMACY: High

RESPONSE: When using an AI tool—especially if it's one you don't pay for—you should be very careful about what information you enter. Avoid entering any sensitive information about your clients, customers, or business. It's unlikely that, by entering Acme Corp's top-secret product road map into ChatGPT, it will be spit out verbatim as soon as someone else asks for it. Still, the terms of service for AI engine agreements typically state that if you don't pay for the plan, they have the right to train their algorithms on your data. And you still need protections in place if you're paying. AI companies are more likely to offer more protections to enterprise customers.

> When using an AI tool—especially if it's one you don't pay for—you should be very careful about what information you enter.

You can get around this, but it requires researching different AI applications and thoroughly reviewing their policies. That means reading the fine print, or enlisting a trusted friend, colleague, lawyer, or adviser who can.

When it comes to using AI to brainstorm more general ideas (like blog post topics), you don't have to worry. The output likely won't be hyperspecific to your business. Additionally, you minimize any risks when your inputs and outputs relate to publicly available information. For instance, if you're using AI to help with competitive reviews and it's based on analyzing competitors' websites (along with your own), then there is unlikely to be any sensitive data or privacy concerns. If you're working on marketing collateral that you share publicly, that's hardly a risk. For the larger AI engines, there's a good chance that much of the open web and many public documents are already in their training data.

3.2 Algorithmic Bias

OBJECTION: Algorithms are trained on biased data, so their outputs are biased too.

LEGITIMACY: Moderate

RESPONSE: The legitimacy can be low, moderate, or high depending on your desired output. Also, algorithmic bias is often improving, especially from the major AI engines that receive the most investment. There is increasing public scrutiny of the output of the engines, and there is growing awareness that bias is an issue that needs to be addressed. There have also been cases of AI engines overcorrecting biases by creating new biases,[20] such as if you request AI to generate an image of a US president from before the year 2000 and it shows only women and people of color. (All US presidents until 2009, when Barack Obama took office, were white men.)

You can test this yourself, and it's most apparent in image generation. You often need to be specific with what you're looking for. If you're creating an image of a crowd, for instance, sometimes, all it takes is saying you want "a diverse crowd," and it'll do the trick. Sometimes, it won't, however, and it might only correct for a factor like race but not account for gender, age, ability, and other factors.

This is also a case of AI often being a mirror of the world and not a distortion of it. AI outputs tend to reflect its inputs.

3.3 High Implementation Costs

OBJECTION: The costs for implementing AI programs are so steep that it's hard to get a high return.

LEGITIMACY: Moderate

RESPONSE: The costs for evaluating, implementing, and rolling out AI depend on what you're doing with it. If you're trying to create your own version of ChatGPT that is only for your organization's use, the cost will not likely be worth it. Stanford University's 2024 "AI Index Report" stated, "According to AI Index estimates, the training costs of state-of-the-art AI models have reached unprecedented levels."[21] Most businesses will not want to try and compete with the big tech players, just like few would want to build their own version of Google search or Microsoft Office.

The good news is that few businesses would even attempt to do such a thing. The off-the-shelf tools, whether for individuals or enterprises, keep getting better. As Greg Shove wrote on No Mercy/No Malice, "For the first time, we can talk to computers in our language and get answers that *usually* make sense. We have a personal assistant and adviser in our pocket, and it costs $20 a month. This is *Star Trek* (58 years ago)—and it's just getting started."[22]

> A lot of ways to implement AI involve process improvements and aligning the right technologies with the right skill sets on your teams.

Many of the best AI technologies have free versions, with subscriptions that cost ten to fifty dollars per month—affordable for most small businesses, especially when this saves time or money, or when it helps you deliver products and services where you can immediately see the return on investment (ROI).

3.4 High Failure Rate

OBJECTION: Corporate AI projects are likely to fail.

LEGITIMACY: High

RESPONSE: The data here points to a worrisome trend: AI projects do seem doomed.

A 2024 report from global policy think tank RAND Corporation said, "By some estimates, more than 80% of AI projects fail—twice the rate of failure for information technology projects that do not involve AI."[23]

These stories have been coming out for years. In 2022, research firm Gartner predicted that "half of finance AI projects will be delayed or canceled by 2024."[24]

Most of these projects are large endeavors at big corporations. These are typically organizations that can overinvest in new technologies, and the degree of complexity is way higher than what most businesses will face.

RAND also noted five reasons for the high failure rate, and being aware of these can help you prepare for the worst so that your projects succeed:

1. People often misunderstand the problems that AI should solve.
2. Organizations training AI models don't have the necessary data. (See "High Implementation Costs" above; this won't come up for most companies.)
3. Companies tend to focus on tapping into the newest technologies rather than solving customers' problems.
4. Organizations don't have the necessary infrastructure.
5. AI is being tapped for challenges that currently surpass the technology's limitations.

Even though failure rates are high, workers tend to value it. Accenture reported that "95% of workers see value in working with gen AI,"[25] LinkedIn said that "4 in 5 people want to learn more about how to use AI in their profession,"[26] and Microsoft found that "79% of leaders agree their company needs to adopt AI to stay competitive."[27] Plus, Google Cloud's study, "The ROI of Gen AI: A Global Survey of Enterprise Adoption and Value," said, "84% of organizations successfully transform a gen AI use case idea into production within six months."[28]

3.5 Skill Gaps

OBJECTION: Your business lacks the specialized knowledge and skills on your team to manage AI implementation.

LEGITIMACY: Moderate

RESPONSE: You may not have all the necessary skills in-house, but you probably have more than you realize, even if you're new to AI. That's because it's getting easier to find AI technologies that complement and augment existing skills, and there are all kinds of resources to help you get a head start.

These days, it seems like practically everyone is an AI expert, or at least this is what they claim on LinkedIn. That's because it is complex to roll out AI projects across organizations, as we've seen with the high failure rate. But we've also seen that people are eager to learn how to use it.

The best way to start closing that skill gap is to encourage experimentation and usage—without compromising company or customer data. Your business or organization may require some outside training or consultation; if you have a budget for professional education, then you can shift some of those resources toward learning about AI.

What you don't need to do is rush out and hire a chief AI officer (CAIO). Just like how the chief digital officer role faded in prominence as everything in the digital bucket got folded into everyone's jobs, most organizations won't need dedicated AI teams. Everyone will need to understand where AI fits in with their roles, and where it doesn't. (See more about this in the next chapter.)

3.6 Lack of Clear ROI

OBJECTION: It's hard to measure the ROI of AI programs, so it's better to stick to what's been done before where the metrics are clearer.

LEGITIMACY: Moderate

RESPONSE: It depends on how you're using AI.

What's the ROI of using a customer relationship management (CRM) system like Salesforce or HubSpot? Most businesses that have sizable prospect and customer databases can't get by without such software. If you've been using spreadsheets to manage your customer list and you start paying for technology that allows you to be one hundred times more productive with that list, it's still difficult to gauge the exact ROI. You make the investments you determine are right for the business. And many AI investments are like that.

Some AI projects have more tangible results. They might allow you to produce ten times the amount of content with the same team, or they might obviate the need for you to hire additional resources. You might be able to use AI to personalize videos for one thousand different people rather than sending the same video to all of them, and that personalized video might be 10 percent more effective, allowing you calculate the returns (or maybe the video is 10 percent less effective—as you saw above, projects often fail).

Read more about measuring the effectiveness of AI programs in chapter 10 on measuring success.

3.7 Integration with Existing Systems

OBJECTION: AI tools may not integrate well with your other marketing platforms, causing operational headaches.

LEGITIMACY: Moderate

RESPONSE: This could be the case, but you'll have to evaluate each technology partner and vendor independently. This will matter for some more than others.

To a large degree, the rich keep getting richer when it comes to AI. Google, Meta, Amazon, and Microsoft have all made massive investments in their own AI technologies. Microsoft is the largest backer of ChatGPT maker OpenAI. Amazon and Google are the two largest investors in Anthropic, which launched Claude. Amazon founder Jeff Bezos is a major backer of Perplexity, which has been hailed at times as a viable alternative to Google's search engine. Adobe has one of the most robust AI-powered creative suites. If you're using products from some of the largest tech players, odds are that you already have access to some of their AI capabilities, and they will try to make their AI capabilities "sticky" enough that you get locked into their systems even more deeply.

There's also the opportunity to break down silos. AI is generally designed to process way more data way faster, so such technologies can suck up tons of information from different sources if you allow for such access. Normalizing reporting has been a longtime source of frustration for marketers, so AI should be able to help give a more unified view into what's working.

Retail and advertising pioneer John Wanamaker was known to have said, "I am convinced that about one-half the money I spend for advertising is wasted, but I have never been able to decide which half."[29] He died more than a century ago; perhaps before another century goes by (or another decade), AI will provide answers to this persistently thorny question.

3.8 Customer Pushback

OBJECTION: The use of AI will alienate customers, so it's better to minimize or covertly deploy AI.

LEGITIMACY: Moderate

RESPONSE: Fear is rarely a healthy reason to avoid doing something, but it's admirable to consider customers' feelings when changing how you operate or go to market. Plus, consumers really will get outraged about anything. Consider the minefield that a furniture retailer stepped in, per *The New York Times*: "So when Ikea casually abandoned its version of the famed 20th-century font Futura that had served it for 50 years and replaced it for 2010 with the computer-screen font Verdana, professional outrage was immense."[30] Yes, changing the catalog font can spark a manufactured crisis. Couldn't AI implementation be worse?

It absolutely could. But that doesn't mean AI should be considered inherently dangerous or untrustworthy.

One factor is that there's a difference between how people respond to surveys and how they act. For instance, a Gartner survey found that nearly two-thirds (64 percent) of customers "would prefer that companies didn't use AI for customer service," citing concerns that AI will make it more difficult to reach an actual human while also displacing humans' jobs.[31] Yet, in practice, there are examples like the "buy now, pay later" company Klarna implementing AI for customer service and consumers rating this as a positive experience.

Many of the applications of AI are never seen by customers or those outside of the company. Few consumers, journalists, or investors have a detailed grasp on exactly how a manufacturer conducts research or prototypes products. For consumers on the receiving end of a company's ad campaign, it's unlikely they'll know how that ad was targeted; it's likely the advertiser or agency doesn't know exactly how that ad was targeted, either, if it was brokered through an automated system.

> AI, like so many technologies, is most effective when it's invisible.

3.9 AI Isn't Just a Tool

There's a comic from cartoonist Tom Fishburne who draws the Marketoonist series where one executive comes into a room with a hammer sporting the word "AI," and he says to his colleagues, who are standing by a table full of giant screws, "I think we may have a solution to all our problems."[32]

If AI is such a hammer and what you need is a screwdriver, don't use it. With the high failure rate of AI projects, it's smart to be skeptical, just like you should be skeptical about whether vendors' AI-powered tools are any different from what they were like before.

AI isn't just a tool, though. It's not even a Swiss Army knife. It's part of the steel that makes up all kinds of tools. It's like digital or mobile; it's everywhere. Just as operating a physical retail store requires different skill sets from operating an e-commerce site,

AI requires new skills. But your focus should be on how to best harness AI, not on whether you should use it at all.

CASE STUDY:
AN AI RECIPE FROM A LEGENDARY HOTEL

Even if you don't know about the Hotel Sacher in Vienna, Austria, you might have heard of its famous dessert, the Sacher-Torte, though the dessert reportedly dates back to 1832, and the hotel opened in 1876.[33]

Think a hotel that guards a secret pastry recipe for two hundred years is stuck in the past? Hardly. And it shows how no brand is too old (or too young) to embrace AI if its team is looking ahead to the future.

Consider the results of a program where the hotel tapped chatbot software maker HiJiffy to use conversational AI for its customer service hub.

In a yearlong period from 2023 to 2024, Hotel Sacher reported:[34]

- 24,300 conversations
- 23,361 conversations fully automated by the chatbot
- 96 percent automation rate
- Estimated 1,200 hours saved by the hotel staff
- On peak days, the app had 130 conversations and referred only two to staff, signaling high customer satisfaction with the automation

The hotel proprietors know that they can't change the recipe for the cake, but they can change their formula to provide world-class service in ways that best serve their customers' needs.

CHAPTER SUMMARY

KEY TAKEAWAYS:

- AI adoption faces legitimate objections. Marketers must distinguish between real risks and misconceptions based on fear to make informed decisions.
- Skepticism is healthy given high failure rates for AI initiatives, so strategic evaluation is key.
- Using AI requires new skills and a learning mindset, so embrace continuous learning and experimentation.
- Your goal shouldn't be to prove AI is useful. It's to make AI work for you and effectively integrate it into your processes.

CHAPTER 4

Selecting and Implementing AI Tools

You shouldn't choose your tools first when incorporating AI into your marketing mix.

Getting into the tools is often the most fun. Join any interactive webinar or panel about AI, and someone (often someone like me) is always saying, "Share in the chat your favorite AI tool right now." It always gets people talking.

And, to be fair, whenever I give a talk about AI and spend too long talking about the strategy, people start nodding off. But when I start showing examples of tools, iPhone flashbulbs start going off so fast that I feel, if only for a moment, like Meghan Markle, Duchess of Sussex (yes, I had to Google both the spelling of her name and her proper title; sometimes, search engines are still faster than AI).

Here's the bad news: This chapter won't get into the specifics of what my favorite tools are and why you should pick one over the other.

Here's the good news: You'll find a lot of those favorites in the online companion. That way, it'll stay current.

And here's the best news: In this chapter, you'll learn how to figure out how to select the right tools for the job.

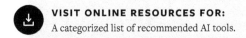

VISIT ONLINE RESOURCES FOR:
A categorized list of recommended AI tools.

4.1 Technology Evaluation Approaches

When evaluating technologies, there are a few routes you can consider.

1. **Tried and true:** The odds are pretty good that companies like Google, Amazon, Meta, Microsoft, and Adobe will still be here a year from now, and probably even a decade from now. Ever hear the phrase, "Nobody ever got fired for buying IBM"? When it comes to AI-powered marketing tools, such companies keep making bigger investments across products that can benefit everyone from solopreneurs to global enterprises. (Ironically, IBM once was arguably the leading brand in AI, back around the time when its Watson technology famously won *Jeopardy!* in 2011. Now, it's unlikely many people would think of it first when naming the leading players in AI.)

2. **Strong pedigree:** For a company that isn't that established, there may be other signs that it will have some staying power. Perhaps it's a company backed by one of the tech giants mentioned above. There might be well-known investors putting in money. The founders could have had a successful run before. It could have celebrity endorsements, which might not mean much but would signal that the founders have a lot of money or connections, or both. If you heard Ryan Reynolds or Oprah was on the board, you might be tempted to take a meeting (admit it: you'd do so just on the off chance you'd wind up on a Zoom with them). None of these factors are guarantees of long-term success, but they can help the odds.

3. **New breakthroughs:** What about taking a chance on something that is new and less tested but meets a need you have? Perhaps the start-up scored some press, and you're itching to see what the buzz is about. Maybe you heard about it from your favorite *Non-Obvious Guide* author (ahem). Most of these start-ups won't be around years from now, but all the companies you have heard of started small at one point. William Hewlett and David Packard were the prototypical "two folks in a garage" when they started their eponymous company in 1938. If you pick the right start-up whose products meet your needs, and the company winds up sticking around, you also have the opportunity to help shape their product road map in a way you never could do with an established tech company.

There are frameworks for incorporating all three approaches. Eric Schmidt, when he was CEO of Google, was credited with implementing a 70-20-10 rule to promote innovation.[35] Google's team members were supposed to manage their time this way:

- 70 percent to core business needs
- 20 percent to projects related to the core
- 10 percent to anything new and unrelated

Coca-Cola, savvy marketers that they were, refined this into a similar framework called Now/New/Next. It's a reminder that most of the time and investment needs to go into meeting the most important needs for the business, but there should always be some resources allocated to new endeavors.[36]

4.2 Key Factors for Evaluating AI

When determining what factors to consider for evaluating new technologies, consider these thirteen factors:

FACTOR 1 **RELEVANCE TO BUSINESS GOALS:** Does it support your objectives? How likely is it to be a solution to your problems, as opposed to a solution in search of a problem?

FACTOR 2 **VALUE FOR YOUR CUSTOMERS:** Will it benefit those who pay for your products or services?

FACTOR 3 **COST:** Does it fit within your budget, or can you make it fit?

FACTOR 4 **ROI:** Is there a way for the investment in such tech to pay for itself, or even turn a profit?

FACTOR 5 **SCALABILITY:** Can it scale with your business, across multiple departments, divisions, or customers?

FACTOR 6 **ECONOMIES OF SCALE:** Do costs scale proportionately as your business uses it more, or does the value increase with usage, incentivizing you to use it as much as possible?

FACTOR 7 **COMPETITIVE ADVANTAGE:** Will this help you keep up with the competition or get ahead of it? If your peers aren't using it, that can be a pro or a con.

FACTOR 8 **RELIABILITY:** Is it used by competitors, peers, or other businesses remotely like yours? Are you comfortable being a guinea pig, or a fast follower? Would you rather have others use the product or the latest features for a while to get the kinks out? There's no right or wrong answer, but you should make sure the stage of the tech fits in with your preferences and risk tolerance.

FACTOR 9 **USABILITY:** How easy is it to learn how to use the tech? Is it intuitive? Are there training materials or onboarding sessions? Can you figure out how to use it *without* an onboarding session? Does it look like a chore to use or a pleasure?

FACTOR 10 **INTEGRATION:** How well does it fit in with other tools you're using? For example, if you're using AI to create outbound marketing messages to specific customer segments, you'll want it to integrate with your customer database. A content writing tool should similarly tie in as smoothly as possible with your content management suite.

FACTOR 11 **PRIVACY AND SECURITY:** Can the AI models of the tech be trained on your data? What happens if you upload info about your business, employees, or customers? Can you trust it? How sensitive is the data that you'll upload to or export from it? What's the worst that can happen? Ask tough questions so you can avoid any pitfalls.

FACTOR 12 **ETHICS AND VALUES:** Does the team behind the product adhere to the ethical standards that align with your business? How are they ensuring it fits in with your priorities and your firm's values?

FACTOR 13 **FUTURE-PROOFING:** What does the road map look like? What are the odds that a well-funded competitor will roll out similar features or better features? How are their revenues, or how well are they funded? What is this company doing to ensure that they're still here a year from now?

4.3 Conducting an AI Audit

How can you determine what tools you need and where AI best fits in?

One way to do this is by auditing your processes and tasks, exploring how automation can help, and tracking the effectiveness.

Yet, in practice, what often happens is this:

- You hear about a new tool in the news or from a friend.
- You check it out further or have a team member do so.
- It looks cool or useful, or it seems like it could give you a competitive advantage.
- You try it out and see how it goes.

In that case, the factors above and the accompanying checklist online can get you far enough along.

If you want to be proactive, though, you'll want to use this AI audit guide, even if it's just for a handful of processes for certain roles in your business. We'll focus on content marketing tasks, which we cover further in chapter 8, since they're relevant to most businesses, but this audit can be used for all disciplines within marketing, and then more widely across other areas of the business.

Here are the five steps to the audit, along with some guides for setting up worksheets. You can also find these on our online resource guide.

STEP ONE: LIST MARKETING TASKS

In the most granular detail possible, list out your marketing tasks. If you have a marketing team, have each one start with all your tasks. Use an AI tool to help you. Without sharing any specific data with an AI engine, you can write a prompt saying, "For someone with the role of X within a company that does Y, come up with a detailed list of tasks that are likely involved."

The task audit can look something like this:

SUBTASKS FOR WRITING BLOG POSTS	FREQUENCY	TIME SPENT PER TASK
Researching topics	Weekly	1 hour
Drafting content	Weekly	2 hours
Editing and proofreading	Weekly	1 hour
Search engine optimization (SEO)	Weekly	30 minutes

SUBTASKS FOR CREATING INFOGRAPHICS	FREQUENCY	TIME SPENT PER TASK
Designing graphics	Monthly	10 hours
Sourcing data	Monthly	2 hours
Writing descriptions	Monthly	2.5 hours

STEP TWO: DETERMINE AUTOMATION POTENTIAL

Once you have your audit, you can review where the automation opportunities lie.

This means adding three more columns:

1. **Can AI automate this?** Consider whether it seems feasible for AI agents or other tools to complete the task. You can list such tools in this column, or you can create another column or tab for specifying them.

2. **Can other automation tools help?** Perhaps you don't need new technology that's specifically AI-related. For instance, if you want help with proofreading, you could use an AI engine, or you could incorporate a tool like Grammarly which has since incorporated AI. Your existing stack may be able to handle much of what's needed.

3. **How much human oversight is required?** Is it labor-intensive to set this up and manage it, or does it allow people to shift their hours elsewhere?

	FREQUENCY	TIME SPENT PER TASK	CAN AI AUTOMATE THIS?	CAN OTHER AUTOMATION TOOLS HELP?	HOW MUCH HUMAN OVERSIGHT IS REQUIRED?
Subtasks for **WRITING BLOG POSTS**					
RESEARCHING TOPICS	Weekly	1 hour	✓ (AI can assist in gathering relevant information)	✓ (Automation for content discovery)	Moderate (input and review)
DRAFTING CONTENT	Weekly	2 hours	✓ (Generative AI can draft initial versions of content)	☒	Moderate to high
EDITING AND PROOFREADING	Weekly	1 hour	✓ (AI can assist with grammar and clarity)	✓ (Automation for basic grammar checks)	Moderate
SEARCH ENGINE OPTIMIZATION (SEO)	Weekly	30 minutes	✓ (AI can analyze and suggest keyword optimizations)	☒	Low
Subtasks for **CREATING INFOGRAPHICS**					
DESIGNING GRAPHICS	Monthly	10 hours	✓ (Generative AI can assist in creating basic designs)	☒	High (depending on how involved the design is)
SOURCING DATA	Monthly	2 hours	✓ (AI can help automate data extraction)	✓ (Automation for data collection)	Low
WRITING DESCRIPTIONS	Monthly	2.5 hours	✓ (AI can assist in drafting descriptions)	☒	Low

STEP THREE: PRIORITIZATION AND OWNERSHIP

The next step is building on this for any tasks that can be automated with a list of tools that could or will be used to automate them, the priority for automating (or partially automating) the task, the action plan for doing so, and the owner. It can look something like this:

TASK NAME	**WRITING BLOG POSTS**
AI/AUTOMATION TOOL	Acme AI Widget
PRIORITY	High
ACTION PLAN	Use AI for first draft of noncritical posts (e.g., evergreen topics); human editor to review and finalize. Avoid AI for posts about the company and our products.
OWNER	Maria S., content marketing manager

STEP FOUR: REVIEW EFFECTIVENESS

Next, you have the review process.

This can go different ways.

One approach is to focus on the time saved by automating various tasks. This works well for organizations and teams that are quantitative and used to time-tracking. There are pros and cons to using time savings as a key performance indicator (KPI); read more about this in chapter 10 where we discuss measurement and metrics. In situations where you're reaping the benefits of automation, it can lead to changes in how you structure teams, your organization, and agency or service provider contracts. Most of the time, though, benefits are incremental rather than transformational. Granted, if you or your organization become 1 percent more efficient each week, that leads to 68 percent more efficiency over the course of the year. And, yes, I had to check that math on three different AI engines.

> Most of the time, benefits from automation are incremental rather than transformational.

Another approach is qualitative. How much peace of mind does it bring you? Does it seem like you're making progress toward your goals? Is your team running better? Do team members seem more energized to have these tools and processes that they can harness? By using AI to help with what's often busywork or tedious jobs, do team members have more time to think strategically, focus on other projects, or connect with each other? Do people feel less overworked? Tangible results from such improvements can be harder to pinpoint but could show up later on.

Below is a way you can track this. You may want to put more emphasis on qualitative versus quantitative approaches based on what works best for your business.

TASK NAME	RESEARCHING TOPICS	DRAFTING CONTENT	EDITING AND PROOFREADING
TIME SPENT BEFORE AUTOMATION	2 hours	3 hours	30 minutes
TIME SPENT AFTER AUTOMATION	45 minutes	1 hour	15 minutes
TIME SAVED	75 minutes	120 minutes	15 minutes
PERCEIVED EFFECTIVENESS (SCALE OF 1–10)	8	9	7

STEP FIVE: MONITOR AND OPTIMIZE

Once you start implementing automation tools, AI-powered or otherwise, continuously monitor their effectiveness. Set a date, such as thirty or ninety days later, to meet with relevant team members and figure out what to do more of, do less of, or change. Expand the process to more tasks and roles as needed.

And, if all of that's overkill, then go ahead and opportunistically evaluate AI tools as they come up. You can still keep that checklist handy to make sure you're considering them the right way.

VISIT ONLINE RESOURCES FOR:
The AI Tool Selection worksheet and the AI Audit and Optimization worksheet.

4.4 AI Leadership and Governance: The Rise of the CAIO

Guess who *isn't* typically owning AI?

You. Or your boss. Or your colleagues in marketing with whom you're empathizing. Or your marketing team, if you are the big boss.

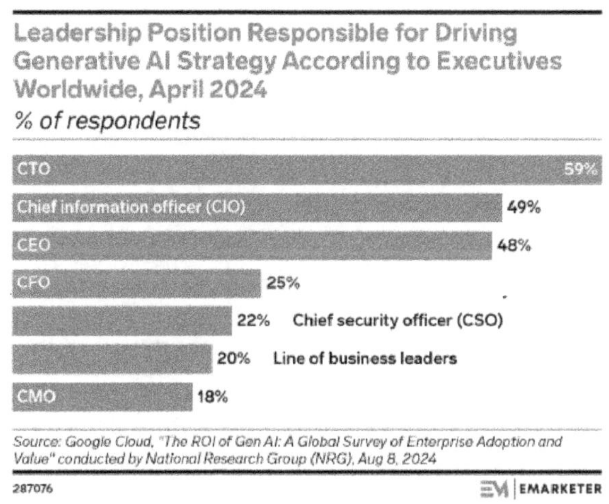

According to a 2024 study by Google Cloud cited by eMarketer, chief marketing officers (CMOs) came in dead last in a list of leadership functions that are "responsible for driving generative AI strategy." Respondents could select more than one option, and chief technology officers (CTOS, 59 percent), chief information officers (CIOs, 49 percent), and chief executive officers (CEOs, 48 percent) all led the pack, followed by finance, security, and then a generic "line of business leaders." Fewer than one-fifth of respondents said the CMO is in charge of generative AI.[37]

There's good reason for this. If your organization is big enough to have a CTO and/or a CIO, then they're the ones who can ensure any AI implementation makes sense from a technical perspective.

> CMOs, however, have the biggest opportunity to deploy AI for external purposes. They can put it to work to directly address customer needs and opportunities.

Even if CTOs and CIOs are driving generative AI strategy, CMOs should be highly sought-after for how to put it to good use—and for what needs it could fill in the first place. (CMOs' counterparts, chief revenue officers, are conspicuously absent in the report, as none of the respondents seemed to have that title, but they would have some useful input as well.)

A common approach for businesses is to have some kind of interdisciplinary AI council or task force to address AI needs. These can incorporate not just the disciplines mentioned above (including sales) but also areas like product management, operations, research and development, and legal. Someone still needs to chair and convene said council, and that more often comes from the tech discipline. If you're a marketer and such a group doesn't exist yet, then you can seize the opportunity.

4.5 Calling All CAIOs

What about having a CAIO leading the charge?

Is this the position of the future? My short answer: I doubt it.

As transformative as AI is, the role of the CAIO sounds like something from organizations in the 1990s that added chief internet officers or chief web officers, or those in the 2000s that added chief digital officers, or those that added chief mobile officers in the 2010s. Some might argue for a CW3O (a chief Web3 officer).

Based on some searches conducted in the fall of 2024, there were about twenty chief Web3 officers on LinkedIn, and there were even eighteen thousand chief digital officers, but that's less than one-tenth of the number of chief marketing officers.[38]

At the same time, 1,300 people come up in a search for CAIOs, and that number is bound to rise. How do you even hire a CAIO? What experience do you look for? It's not like there are many VPs of AI whom you can poach or promote.

I was going to do some research into where these CAIOs come from, assuming they were previously CTOs or CIOs who had their titles enhanced. Then, on the very first result that I clicked, the CAIO's previous experience was serving as a Brazilian jujitsu instructor—I kid you not.

What will likely happen is a spike and then a gradual drop-off of these CAIO titles. Many will list handling AI among their responsibilities, but AI will be such a seamless part of processes, channels, and tactics that it will be like another element—one that it will be hard to survive without.

Some say the CAIO role is likely to endure. Palmer Group CEO Shelly Palmer, a longtime strategist, pundit, practitioner, and instructor, tackled this in his column entitled, "Do You Need a Chief AI Officer (CAIO)?"

Palmer wrote, "In most of our client companies, all of the C-Suite tech roles are already full time, highly specialized jobs. Could a CEO form an AI committee including all of the other tech leaders? Of course. But a CAIO, fully dedicated and focused on the unique challenges and opportunities presented by AI, makes great sense . . . By having a CAIO, organizations can ensure that AI initiatives have a focused leader who can advocate for and manage the complexities of AI technology, from ethical considerations to integration across various business units. As AI continues to evolve, the CAIO's role will only grow in relevance and importance, making it a pivotal position in any forward-thinking company's leadership team."[39]

Palmer has a great point.

If you are considering adding a CAIO role, here's a quick roundup of the pros and cons of the role, particularly as it pertains to marketing:

	PROS OF HIRING CAIO	**CONS OF HIRING CAIO**
AGILITY	Can focus on pushing through AI initiatives	Adds another decision-maker that can slow plans down when there's disagreement
EXPERTISE	Can ensure various disciplines' needs are met, including those of the CMO	More likely to come from a technical background that might not fully account for a CMO's priorities
RISK MANAGEMENT	Helpful for understanding risks associated with any AI initiatives and new technologies	For marketers, there's often danger both in being risk-averse and risk-tolerant, so it'll be important to find that middle ground
COMPETITIVE ADVANTAGE	A CAIO's center of excellence, if funded well, can turn a pipeline of innovative projects into an edge that peers can't match	Getting bogged down in too many pilots could be a distraction

RESOURCE ALLOCATION	A CAIO might be able to muster more resources for high-impact projects	Those resources have to come from somewhere, so how much do you want the marketing budget to fund it?
COLLABORATION	With the CAIO, the organization can get a new center of excellence that communicates across departments and improves the spread of knowledge among them	A CAIO could also preside over yet another silo where projects succeed or fail based on the AI team alone

CHAPTER SUMMARY

KEY TAKEAWAYS:

- When evaluating technologies, there are a few routes to consider: the tried and true, those with a strong pedigree, and the new breakthroughs.
- Choosing AI tools should be driven by strategy, not technology. Identify business goals and needs before selecting a tool.
- The 70-20-10 rule helps balance AI tool selection. Use a mix of established solutions, emerging tools, and experimental innovations to balance out risk.
- Auditing marketing processes helps determine where AI can create the most impact. List marketing tasks, explore the potential for automation, and evaluate the priority level.
- AI tools should be regularly assessed for effectiveness as technologies evolve.
- While CTOs and CIOs are generally the people driving AI implementation, CMOs have the biggest opportunity to deploy AI for external purposes to directly address customer needs.

PART TWO

Putting AI to Work

CHAPTER 5

Developing AI-Infused Marketing Strategies

Here's a little secret you need to understand about AI, especially when it comes to marketing (but it applies more broadly):

> With AI, you don't need to be as good a writer, but you need to be a better editor.

As someone who's been writing long-form content since age six (I kid you not; you should have seen my first book report on *Stuart Little*, aided by my word processor's thesaurus), that is painful to admit.

It should be a relief for you if writing isn't your thing. But it should also be what keeps you up at night. Sometimes, you need to be a *very* good editor to make AI work for you.

When I say "writer" and "editor" here, I'm referring to those roles in the broadest possible terms. For writers, it refers to any creative act, and "creative" refers to anything you can create—even if it's something like a spreadsheet that you don't think of as being particularly creative.

When I say "editor," I'm referring to someone who reviews and improves the work. Maybe that includes literal editing skills. But it could entail other acumens, like having an eye for whether an image or video is on-brand and exceeds a client's expectations.

This is because AI is generally very good at writing first drafts, and it's not usually so good at writing final drafts.

If you give AI better inputs (like examples of your past work, your company's style guides, or sales collateral), then AI can potentially deliver better first drafts.

You still need to treat all AI outputs as first drafts.

Once you use any AI tool with that mindset, you're ready to take advantage of it.

5.1 You Don't Need an AI Marketing Strategy

Now that you're ready to start, do you need an AI marketing strategy?

No, for one simple reason:

There's no such thing as an AI marketing strategy. There's just marketing strategy, and it doesn't matter what tools you use to devise or execute it.

It's the same lesson I learned while working on 360i's *Social Marketing Playbook* that I referenced in the introduction. The strategy should work regardless of the specific tools and channels involved.

There is one way to factor in AI:

> Use your knowledge about AI to expand your thinking about what you want your marketing strategy to achieve.

Say you're taking part in a weekly conference call with your favorite AI community, and you learn about how there are tools to create video avatars that can deliver personalized messages with customized scripts to each of your customers based on what you know of their behaviors, preferences, and purchase histories. (Yes, such tools exist, and I can't get enough of them, creepy as they often are.)

That doesn't mean you now need some video avatar strategy, or a strategy around that specific tool—just like no one needed a Facebook or Amazon strategy.

But, if you're considering how to increase engagement with your current customers, and you like this idea (even if it makes you a little uncomfortable), now you can add personalized video to the possibilities of what you can do.

On the one hand, using personalized video (especially with any one tool) is super tactical. It doesn't even belong in the same breath as "strategy." Any dyed-in-the-wool marketing strategist (there are many on the farm I come from) would be cringing reading this.

On the other hand, that one product demo could trigger a slew of ideas that weren't on your radar before. Maybe you weren't doing anything to engage customers once they became your customers. Or maybe personalization never crossed your mind.

A demo like that can expand your thinking, even strategically.

And, if you wind up in that gray area that lives between strategies and tactics, and you're not even sure which is which, don't worry about it. No one cares except those dyed-in-the-wool marketing strategists, and in this case, they need to chill.

So now you have a sense of how it works. Write once, edit twice. Don't create an AI marketing strategy. Look for where AI can expand your thinking and achieve your goals.

5.2 Ways to Incorporate AI into Marketing Strategies

With those in mind, here are twenty-one areas where AI can be incorporated into marketing strategies:

MARKET RESEARCH: Analyze market trends and competitor activities, or compile findings based on focus groups and interviews. AI can help broadly and deeply here, from giving suggestions on what questions to ask to analyzing key takeaways from a sweeping series of interviews.

CUSTOMER SEGMENTATION AND TARGETING: Have AI analyze data and create customer segments based on behaviors, segments, and preferences. (See chapter 6 on optimizing customer personas for more information.)

CRM: Track and manage interactions with customers and prospects.

CUSTOMER LOYALTY PROGRAMS: Personalize rewards and recommended offers based on each consumer's purchase history, preferences, and churn risk.

CUSTOMER FEEDBACK: Mine explicit and implicit findings from customer sentiments, and see how that tracks with broader trends across your competitors and category. Determine what issues need to be prioritized to improve feedback.

6

EMAIL MARKETING: Personalize and automate much of the email communication flow. You can also use AI to set up logic for how to respond to people and to intelligently route messages to the right humans. Email marketing is a great conduit to distribute various kinds of AI-generated or AI-assisted content.

7

DIRECT MAIL: Customize mail content and targeting based on signals hidden in customer data. Direct-mail marketers have been using sophisticated targeting methods for years, but AI allows for more advanced forms of targeting and personalization.

8

CHATBOTS AND VIRTUAL ASSISTANTS: Provide instant, targeted customer service and support through text, photos, and video.

9

EVENT MARKETING: Customize invitations based on previous interactions and other data. Create customized, shareable multimedia content for each participant at the event. Send personalized follow-ups to each attendee.

10

DIGITAL OUT-OF-HOME (DOOH) ADVERTISING: Place the right ads on the right digital displays that match best with your company and message. Flight your campaigns to run at optimal times.

11

RETAIL MEDIA: Use AI-powered kiosks or apps to provide personalized product recommendations. Determine which offers should be placed on which displays.

12

AD TARGETING AND OPTIMIZATION: Generate media plans, automatically adjusting bids and targeting while layering in personalization.

13

SOCIAL MEDIA MARKETING: Come up with the idea schedule, optimize distribution, and monitor results.

SEARCH ENGINE OPTIMIZATION (SEO): AI is a double-edged sword here, as it gives with one hand and takes away with the other. All of the added noise generated by AI-generated content makes SEO harder, and optimizing content for AI algorithms presents a slew of new challenges.

TV AND RADIO ADS: Customize ads on the fly (with specified, approved parameters) that relate to the nature of what happened during scripted or live programming. You can expect far more personalization of such ads, though consumers may bristle at ads that seem to know too much about them.

WEBSITE PERSONALIZATION: Dynamically generate custom versions of a website or landing page for each visitor based on their digital behavior and any first-party data you have about them. Can you imagine if every visitor to your site saw the version of it most relevant to them? AI can make that possible. But there are dangers to this, too. If every page is personalized, and perhaps created on the fly, there's no single "source of truth" for people to refer to. Plus, algorithms might alienate customers when making the wrong assumptions.

INFLUENCER MARKETING: Identify the perfect influencers for a given brand and campaign, and then have AI manage many of the steps along the way. Developments in AI have also led to a whole new genre: virtual influencers.

MEDIA MIX MODELING: Determine the right frequency and reach across channels and media properties online and offline, enhanced with more powerful and accurate predictive analytics.

LEAD SCORING AND NURTURING: Assess leads based on their likelihood to convert, prioritize follow-up communications, and automate outreach.

CONTENT CREATION AND CURATION: AI can assist with generating text, images, audio, and video, while also curating content from your own materials or other sources. (See chapter 8 for way more information.)

PREDICTIVE ANALYTICS: Forecast sales trends, customer behaviors, and inventory needs. If there's enough historical data, you can probably use predictive analytics. Be prepared for unexpected events, such as the "black swans" that Nassim Nicholas Taleb has written about, to upend any prediction.[40]

CASE STUDY: BECK'S DRAFTS AI-GENERATED BEER

When Beck's decided to experiment with AI for creating a new kind of beer, it looked for every possible way to include AI.[41]

AI was involved in:

Kickoff conversation: AI was the brainstorming partner.

Idea selection: AI came up with the idea for an AI-generated beer.

Crafting the recipe: AI determined the right blend of yeast, malt, water, and hops.

Naming the product: AI came up with Autonomous.

Writing a brand manifesto: AI gave the brand a strong point of view.

Logo design: AI took all the previous assets as inspiration for the Autonomous logo.

Tagline development: AI's idea was, "The beer that made itself."

Can design: AI created a futuristic look for the product.

Website design: AI designed the website that further brought the product to life.

Creating the ad campaign: AI came up with posters, billboards, and social media ads.

Producing the radio ad: AI both wrote and voiced the radio ad.

Video script: AI wrote the full script to properly tell the Autonomous story.

Influencer selection: AI drafted the influencer strategy, including specific lines that the influencers should use.

Launching the product: Humans may have helped tie it all together and bring Autonomous into the real world, but AI was instrumental every step of the way.

The sales may not be staggering, as Beck's only created 450 limited-edition beers that were sold in select European markets; the beer did quickly sell out.

Beck's Marketing Director Laura Salway said in a statement reported by *Food Dive*, "After being at the forefront of the brewing world for 150 years, this represents the next step in our journey. It's been fascinating to see Beck's Autonomous come to life and how we can continue to embrace new technology in the industry and across brand communications."[42]

CHAPTER SUMMARY

KEY TAKEAWAYS:

- With AI, you don't need to be a good writer, but you need to be a better editor. Success comes from refining, personalizing, and contextualizing AI outputs.
- AI is often very good at writing first drafts, and it's not usually so good at final drafts.
- Your marketing strategy should drive AI adoption, not the other way around.
- AI can expand creative thinking and improve decision-making. Use AI to generate new ideas, test campaign elements, and analyze customer insights for better results.

CHAPTER 6

Optimizing Customer Personas and Personalization with AI

Who is the target of your marketing?

This is one of the most fundamental questions you need to answer, as without it, everything else is likely to fall apart.

When creating a marketing plan and putting that plan in market, you can't conjure up every possible prospect and customer. A high-powered, enterprise-grade AI engine might be able to keep millions of data points about a practically infinite number of people in its memory; as humans, we can't operate like that. It can be tough to remember how many kids or siblings one of our closest colleagues has.

Humans, however, are really good at heuristics, or shortcuts. And that's where personas fit in.

6.1 Customer Personas and AI

Personas give us the gist about people, with enough color to make it feel like we know who we're dealing with. And, once we have that color, we can do something humans are way better at than AI: we can tell stories.

For example, we know that Jamal is a chief financial officer for a community bank in the Midwest. We know that Cosima's plant manufactures agricultural equipment, and she's a road warrior, selling that equipment to industrial farms across most of the Southeast. And we know that Sofia is a doctor, a mom of two, and a chocoholic.

Actually, we don't know any of these things because they're not real people. Using a mix of quantitative and qualitative research tools, along with intuitively understanding your own prospects and customers, you create these personas to represent the much wider set of real people who you want to influence with your marketing.

Full details of persona development are outside the scope of this *Non-Obvious Guide* (you'll find it in *The Non-Obvious Guide to Marketing and Branding*), but you can get the gist of how personas help you understand your target audience.

> One of the most powerful ways to use AI for marketing is to help with customer persona development or enrichment.

This is one of those "make or break" steps. Once you start using AI as a copilot, you will likely keep returning to it. It's one of those tactics that feels like the embodiment of those games that advertise that it takes "a minute to learn, a lifetime to master."

Where exactly does AI fit in with all of this? Let us count the ways:

1. **AI enhances existing personas.** If you've already developed personas, AI can fill in examples and give you a more complete picture. AI can also adapt the information you have into usable formats.

   Say you have a detailed research report about the different personas you're focused on. You can use AI to condense that information with a prompt such as this: "Take each of the personas here, and give me a one-line summary about each one, plus a maximum of five bullet points with a maximum of twenty words per bullet, that describes their most salient traits." You can then take that information and quickly create a slide for each persona that is easily digestible for your teams, clients, or agencies.

2. **AI makes your personas interactive.** If you already have a persona, or you just used AI to create one, you can bring it to life by asking it questions. Using the example of Cosima above, you can tell the AI engine that it will be playing the role of Cosima with the traits identified in the persona, and then ask away:

   "What is a typical day like for you?"

   "How do you stay informed about your industry?"

   "What are some of the biggest pain points you have?"

   "How can the marketing team help you do your job better?"

   "Would you respond better to a direct, clear sales pitch, or a soft sell that eases you into the process?"

   "What's your favorite way to unwind?"

   None of this is going to be scientific, but it can help make your persona feel more "alive," you can brainstorm the kinds of questions you want answered by your actual prospects and customers, and you can start comparing the fictional responses to actual ones once you get more information. If you're stuck on what to ask, have your AI engine recommend more questions.

3. **AI creates your personas based on relevant information.** What if you don't have a persona, or anything resembling one? Maybe you don't know where to begin.

   That's OK. AI can take a first pass for you. And it might even do a half-decent job.

As usual with generative AI, the better your input, the better your output. Some AI engines can scan a website, so you could use that as a starting point. If you've put together any marketing or sales materials, you can upload those.

4. **AI invents your persona from scratch.** Maybe you don't have any materials ready. Maybe you're still in the ideation stage for a new business or project. That's fine, too. Give AI as much of the "what" as you can, and it will produce the "who."

   Read through it. See if it feels right. If it passes that "good enough" threshold, you probably saved weeks worth of analysis—all when what you really need is a gist.

5. **AI creates images for your personas.** Sometimes, it's better to leave more to the imagination. In a way, wasn't reading *The Hunger Games* more fun before everyone around the world pictured the hero as Jennifer Lawrence? No offense to Ms. Lawrence and the abundantly talented cast of the films, but having an actor's face on the book jacket can ruin some of our individual interpretations.

   For personas, you may not want to focus too hard on conjuring what they look like as if you're a sketch artist working on a criminal case. After all, personas are composite sketches as is. But it can be fun to have images for a team to rally around and identify with, maybe even keeping the images on their office or home office desks as reminders.

   It can be a fun exercise to have an AI image generation tool create persona images. For a general AI engine that's multimodal (in this case, it'd be one that can generate both text and images), you can paste in some or all of the text persona and ask it to create a visual. For a specific image creation tool, you might have to format the prompt more succinctly and precisely—and a general AI engine can help you craft such a prompt.

6.2 Applied Persona Development

Once you create the personas, how can you use them?

1. **Lead generation:** Search for prospects that line up with the details of the persona. Use filters based on the persona when searching on platforms such as LinkedIn, and reach out with a targeted, personalized message. If your targets spend time in a forum such as Reddit, use the persona to guide which subreddits (specifically themed channels on Reddit) to target. Want to prioritize an event partnership for sponsorship or speaking? Make sure it's one that your persona would actually go to. Personas can help your team align around tactics: "This is a perfect fit for Ramon." "Niketa would never go there; let's pass." AI engines can help surface some of these recommendations.

2. **Audience segmentation:** As you amass more data about how your personas reflect your customers and prospects, you'll be able to create segments based on their behaviors. These are tasks where AI engines and

specialized AI-powered segmentation tools increasingly excel. You'll likely unearth new segments that can be as straightforward as "Gen Z, married, double-income soccer fans," or more playful, like "single-dad Swifties."

3. **Customer journey mapping and content personalization:** First, you can analyze all the different points of interaction your company has with prospects and customers. Through AI, you can amass and analyze way more data than was typically possible before, and you can get more real-time information about these journeys. Then, you can personalize content to different personas and segments as you take people along the journey that you craft.

> Personas can play a role in so much of your marketing, and as you work with them more, they often become an integral part of how you understand your target audience.

INTERVIEW:
NICHOLA QUAIL, FOUNDER AND CEO OF INSIGHTS EXCHANGE

WHAT AREAS IN AI ARE MOST EXCITING FOR YOU RIGHT NOW?

Nichola Quail: In terms of human research and consumer insights, the area that we're really focusing on is how to ensure that people don't get carried away with going all-in on AI and then forgetting that, without primary data, primary human data, it can go a little awry.

WHAT'S YOUR PERSPECTIVE ON WORKING WITH SYNTHETIC AUDIENCES VERSUS ENGAGING REAL HUMANS FOR INSIGHTS?

Quail: I have many thoughts. We've been working with virtual customer personas and a couple of platforms with and without human data, and just letting it pull from the model that it's been trained on. What we've found is that bias is still inherent in the training models, and that comes out. So, when you're asking for representative insights or representative human personas, unless it's been trained on primary research data, it's just feeding off whatever's found on the internet, and that's not always representative. What we're saying is, with gen AI, please don't take it at face value. It takes a lot of manual work by experienced researchers to really massage the outputs to ensure that it is representative. If you don't have a human benchmark, that's where the danger is.

CAN MARKETERS CREATE GREAT CAMPAIGNS WITH AI?

Quail: Say you've got a marketer that has to create a campaign that's really compelling, that really resonates, or has a unique, emotional hook. If all you've done is rely on data that you've never been involved in because it's AI-generated, and you haven't had any human research experts involved, every campaign and every idea will become very generic and very bland. That's where you miss out on those human emotional nuances.

SO AI ISN'T EVERYTHING.

Quail: With everything that we're doing, AI has become a valuable tool, but it's not the only tool. It goes back to the basics. It's almost like first principles. You know, what do people value? What are their needs? It's the Maslow hierarchy of needs, and most people don't even get to the top with self-actualization. They're very happy about halfway up and aren't necessarily looking to go higher.

CHAPTER SUMMARY

KEY TAKEAWAYS:

- One of the most fundamental questions you need to answer is, *Who is the target of your marketing?* Without it, everything else will likely fall apart.
- AI enhances persona development by analyzing vast amounts of data. This can be used to refine, segment, and personalize marketing efforts.
- AI-generated personas can be interactive, evolving with new insights. Marketers can update persons dynamically based on real-time data and behavior.
- Personalization at scale is one of AI's biggest strengths and opportunities. AI can efficiently help tailor messages and offers to different customers and segments.
- AI should complement human insights, not replace them.
- AI can enhance existing personas, make personas interactive, use relevant information to create personas, invent personas from scratch, and create images for your personas.
- Personas can play a role in so much of your marketing, and as you work with them more, they often become an integral part of how you understand your target audience.

CHAPTER 7

AI-Powered Customer Service and Retention

7.1 How Marketing Can Help Customer Service

Marketers often don't focus on customer service.

One reason is that the marketing role is often focused on bringing in new customers. Once the sale is made or the lead is transferred to the sales team, the marketer's job is done. The structure of a team or organization tends to keep marketing and customer service in separate silos so that, even if a marketer did want to support the customer service team, there wouldn't be a direct line of communication.

> Good marketing can't fix poor customer service, just like good marketing can't fix a shoddy product.

No matter how catchy Apple's ads have been, they'd have been wasted if iPhones were essentially electronic paperweights.

But good marketing can make customer service jobs easier by better communicating the value proposition of what they're promoting and preventing consumer confusion. And customer service can make marketers' jobs easier by sharing data with the marketing team to influence the messaging. If the maker of a unisex T-shirt kept getting calls just from women saying the shirt didn't fit them well, the marketing team could market it as a shirt for men until the product team came up with a truly unisex fit.

Generative AI may prove to be transformative with customer service, largely because people are already used to dealing with automated customer service systems both as chatbots and on the phone. As we'll see in the Klarna case study, people will be happy to deal with a bot to solve customer service issues—as long as it actually resolves situations.

What's new with generative AI is that AI-powered customer service solutions can learn way faster and deploy those findings immediately. There's more room to understand nuance in customers' requests, and also understand varieties of phrases.

Earlier versions of chatbots needed to be programmed for every possibility, explicitly telling the bot that "How are you?", "What's up?", "How's it going?", and "What's going on?" all mean the same thing. Now, AI engines are exponentially more robust, so the focus needs to shift to make sure the bots aren't hallucinating (making stuff up).

7.2 How AI Enhances and Transforms Customer Interactions

There are so many ways that AI is changing customer service, and as AI models become smarter, they'll be capable of handling a greater variety of customers' needs.

Here are some of the areas to consider if you're applying AI in this field. For simplicity, I'm referring to the customer throughout this section, but note that it applies to prospects as well—especially for prospects who have interacted with your business before (that way, you might have some data about them).

1. **Personalized responses based on customer history:** Learn from past exchanges with the customer and adapt messages accordingly, saving the customer time and speaking to them in their language.
2. **Omnichannel personalization:** Personalize how you deliver support across channels based on the customer's preferences, whether it's by phone, email, social media DMs, or chatbots.

The bots themselves can be a mix of text, voice, and video based on preferences.

3. **Proactive responses based on historical data:** Are there patterns that show when certain customers are going to have certain needs addressed? Proactively offer remedies to extend customer lifetime value.
4. **Tailored upsells and cross-sells:** Use opportunities for customer interactions to make recommendations tailored to their purchase history, interests, and behaviors.
5. **Dynamic pricing:** This is always a controversial topic, as pricing that changes per customer and per situation often means the business has the upper hand in maximizing profits. But this is hardly a new concept; anyone who has called a rep to inquire about a cable or phone bill knows that reps have some leeway to offer custom packages that are designed to either acquire a customer or prevent churn. Bots just may be able to do this more effectively at scale, without the customer needing to ask to speak to a manager. Also, expect there to be more bots that game the system for customers. For example, DoNotPay has been a "consumer champion" bot-based service since 2015 and then added an AI layer to enhance effectiveness.[43]
6. **Adapt communication styles based on customer interactions:** What if the form and format of service changed based on the customer's style? Some people may need more hand-holding, while others might appreciate support that's direct and concise so the customer can shift to self-service mode.
7. **Smart FAQs personalized to the customer:** Instead of having one FAQ page for everyone, the order and even specific responses can change based on the customer's history and

behavior. Someone who just spent ten minutes on pricing pages, for instance, would first see different FAQs than someone who was looking at product specifications.

8. **Sentiment analysis:** Human call center reps may be best at picking up on cues of the customer's mood, often with a need to defuse tension and turn a negative experience into a positive (or at least neutral) one. AI is getting better, and such technology may be able to pick up on signals that most humans can't.

9. **Optimized timing for human-to-human support:** So many AI developments benefit from that human-in-the-loop concept. In customer service, that concept is more familiar than in other fields, as even more basic chatbots have been programmed in the past to get a human rep on the line when the customer hits a wall with automated responses. With AI, the promise is that bots can expand the breadth of who can be serviced and the depth of bot-to-human interactions, saving human reps for more intractable problems (or for the human customers who just need to deal with a fellow sentient being, even if it takes longer to complete the task).

10. **Personalized onboarding and product education:** If your product or service requires training, AI can help get a better, faster intake that covers the customer's experience and needs, and then it can customize the journey accordingly. Even the tips that show up can be personalized to the customer. Rather than offering the same ten tips that show up for all users, regardless of their familiarity with the product, tips can very per user—and also adapt based on customer preferences for text, audio, or video.

INTERVIEW:
JEREMIAH OWYANG, GENERAL PARTNER OF BLITZSCALING VENTURES

What Happens When the Customer Is an AI Agent?

DO YOU EXPECT EVERYONE ONLINE TO HAVE SOME KIND OF AI AGENT REPRESENTING THEM? HOW WIDESPREAD WILL THIS PHENOMENON BE, AND HOW FAST IS IT COMING?

Jeremiah Owyang: Yes, everyone will have their own AI agent(s) representing them. There will be at least two categories: one offered by their tech giant of choice (like Apple, Google, Microsoft, Meta, or Amazon), and another category of premium versions from independent AI start-ups. These start-ups will offer customized AI agents that can traverse all digital ecosystems and walled gardens to manage online tasks and gather information.

WHAT WILL CHANGE FOR MARKETERS WHEN THEY'RE TARGETING AGENTS INSTEAD OF PEOPLE?

Owyang: Marketers are well equipped to make this shift. In the Web2 era [epitomized by the rise of social networks], marketers had to transition from influencing press, media, and analysts to also influencing a new cohort of influencers, including their customers using social media and the new influencer profession. Just as they added new cohorts to influence, they will need to add yet another: AI agents. AI agents will make decisions on behalf of human buyers, and marketers will use their own brand-side agents to communicate directly with consumer-side agents and influence them.

CASE STUDY: KLARNA'S CUSTOMER SERVICE SUCCESS

Klarna, a global payment service known for powering many merchants' "buy now, pay later" options, released a customer service assistant in 2024 powered by OpenAI, makers of ChatGPT.

Within one month of it going live globally, the assistant had 2.3 million conversations—two-thirds of Klarna's customer service interactions, or the equivalent of the work of 700 full-time representatives. It led to a 25 percent drop in repeat inquiries and was on track to drive $40 million in profit improvement for the year.[44]

Sebastian Siemiatkowski, cofounder and CEO of Klarna, said, "We are incredibly excited about this launch, but it also underscores the profound impact on society that AI will have."[45]

What remains to be seen is how profoundly positive or negative the impact will be if customer service interactions improve but at the expense of significant job displacement in such fields.

CHAPTER SUMMARY

KEY TAKEAWAYS:

- Marketing and customer service should work together, but they often operate in silos. AI can help bridge the gap.
- Good marketing can't fix poor customer service, just like good marketing can't fix a shoddy product.
- Generative AI is transforming customer service through AI-powered chatbots and virtual assistants that resolve customers' issues faster.
- AI helps deliver personalized customer service at scale, anticipating customers' needs and giving tailored solutions.
- Customer expectations around AI are evolving as customers learn to appreciate its speed and convenience.

CHAPTER 8

AI in Content Creation

When generative AI found its mass market starting in late 2022, the first experiences for most professionals and consumers involved content creation.

Marketers started using such tools to generate content ideas and blog posts. Consumers started creating meal plans. Parents and caretakers created personalized bedtime stories for their children. There was a brief fad where it seemed like everyone was generating crazy selfies, making them look like astronauts or Vikings or werewolves. Things got weird.

And then, on the marketing front, we got to work in earnest, and AI tools immediately started to have an impact on content workflows. MediaPost, reporting on AI Marketers Guild's 2024 member survey, wrote, "In fact, nearly three quarters (73%) of the marketing exec respondents said they already are using AI for text-based content generation, while two-thirds (65%) are using it explicitly to generate images, video and or editing such content."[46]

We'll break down the content creation process and see how AI can and should fit in.

8.1 Research

What is it you want to know? Perhaps you're a subject-matter expert looking to go deeper, or maybe you need to learn about a totally new field.

AI'S ROLE: AI isn't just a helpful educator that you can talk to; it's a great role-player. Have a pitch coming up to the chief data officer of a major credit card company? Tell your AI engine to assume that role, and then ask about what kinds of content interests them.

> Beware of hallucinations here; you don't want to become a subject-matter expert yourself only to base your expertise on made-up facts.

8.2 Ideation

This can start with a blank page, where you have no clue what you're going to be doing and need to brainstorm from scratch. Or you could have some starting points where you need more ideas, better ideas, or both.

AI'S ROLE: AI engines can be useful brainstorming partners.

Here's one thing they have in common with humans, though: most of the ideas aren't very good. It will be your job (or another human's) to determine that.

> AI tools can generate an infinite number of ideas, and they can cover any topic.

8.3 Medium Selection

What format should you use? Should you create a video? A text-heavy social post? A white paper? Could it be a podcast? Will it be a one-off, or a series of Instagram posts or stories?

AI'S ROLE: AI can help determine the right formats to reach your target audience. You'll probably already have a good idea of the right kind of medium for the story you want to tell. This is often determined by a mix of the resources available, what resonates with your target audience, and the expertise of your team (including external resources like freelancers and agencies).

8.4 Channel Selection

How will you distribute the content you create? Will it lend itself better to social media, email, mobile, or various traditional channels? You may know this already—you might be creating content for your blog or emailing attendees who visit your booth at a trade show. But channel selection sometimes is more open-ended.

AI'S ROLE: Like with medium selection, AI's role will be more modest here. It can help determine the best channels for a given target audience, and it can also help with channel expansion when you are set with one channel but want to figure out how to prioritize others. Also, AI engines that have the most up-to-date information and that can search the web for real-time updates can help put together a media plan with the best distribution targets.

8.5 Style and Tone

What does your content sound like? Look like? Feel like? If someone saw one piece of content from you and another from your closest competitor, and there were no logos on either, would it be clear whose was whose? What's the vibe that you're achieving?

AI'S ROLE: You might have strong brand guidelines and identity documents in place already, obviating the need for AI assistance or further human intervention. Often, though, the style and tone could use a refresh, and AI can play a role if you're game. Various AI engines are very good at reverse engineering style from existing documents, and then you can use that to guide other work. Other tools can essentially do the same with your company logo, taking those colors and creating a visual style guide.

You can also use AI for one of my favorite activities: figuring out what kind of celebrity or public figure you want to use as a reference for your tone of voice. Having such a reference that your team can relate to can provide an easy lens to keep in mind, and AI can offer astute suggestions that you can keep refining until you get it right.

8.6 Production

Sooner or later, we are going to get into the content creation itself.

AI'S ROLE: It's a big one. Or a small one. You'll need to decide how you want to involve AI. You might try to avoid it entirely or outsource the whole job to the bots.

How much do you want to rely on AI-generated content? There are a lot of factors to consider:

- **How important is it for you to own the intellectual property?**

> It's possible that you won't have ownership of what you create with AI, and that could be an issue for everything, whether it's a company name, your tagline, product announcements, or thought leadership.

To the extent that this matters to you, you'll have to look up the terms for the service you use and the pricing tier you're on (free plans tend to come with less ownership rights), and for more critical business needs, you should consult a lawyer.

- **How effective are the tools for generating it?** An AI tool designed to create something straightforward like a text-based search ad will more likely be reliable than a tool that tries to create perspectives in your voice that you can share on LinkedIn. Video is often orders of magnitude more complex for AI to handle than still images. For instance, the default frame rate for videos shot on iPhones (and many other devices) is 30 frames per second, so one minute of video has 1,800 frames to process. That requires a lot of computing power, and it creates a lot of opportunities for things to go wrong with AI.

- **How much can you supervise the AI?** Do you have the right team members to review the content and make sure it's accurate and on-brand? There's a funny paradox where the more skilled the humans managing the AI are, the more you can rely on AI to do the job well. The degree of supervision needed can also vary based on the sensitivity of what you're doing and how critical it is for your business. For instance, a press release that you're putting out about your company so you can tout a new product feature on your blog isn't usually going to require as much handling and editing as an announcement about landing your newest and biggest client where you have the client speaking on the record.
- **How scalable is AI for your content creation needs?** What does AI need to accomplish to achieve the content goals that you're establishing? How much time (or resources) needs to be saved, and how much high-quality content needs to be generated? Resources are an important factor here, too, as you need to be able to supervise AI at scale if a massive amount of content is being generated. If you have global or localized content, you'll need to be able to assess the quality of AI-created content in all of those contexts, too, and ensure that it all adheres to your same quality standards.
- **What are the odds of hallucinations?** AI will likely be better at generating content that relates to tons of examples that it has seen before, such as how to change a tire. If you ask AI for something less common, like how to

convert your car into a hovercraft, it will probably fill in a lot of blanks with guesswork. You'd be surprised at how AI can seemingly screw up simple requests, even when it can generate entire worlds from scratch. For instance, I often find that AI engines are horrible at counting words in a block of text, and then when I press it to adjust it to, say, under fifty words or five hundred characters, it botches the assignment.

Another one that a friend, Gene Keennan, told me about that is constantly true any time I try it is asking an image generator to show you a picture of a wooden wagon wheel with three spokes. This might be fixed at some point, but I spent months trying this, and a series of different AI apps consistently failed. The reason why is fascinating:

> AI is great at generating content based on its training data, but it's terrible at making things up that it hasn't seen before.

Apparently, no AI engine has seen a wooden wheel with such few spokes. If you're going to try and create something entirely new, that's a much harder problem for AI, and it'll likely be faster to find a designer on Fiverr who can do the job.

We can also expect consumer tolerance for AI hallucinations to grow over time as people get used to AI's quirks and as AI's accuracy increases. As Pete Pachal wrote in his newsletter for The Media Copilot, "The take of, 'Don't use AI because it sometimes makes mistakes,' doesn't really hold water anymore. It's such a useful tool that we'll simply take that into account."[47]

- **What are other risks for using AI-generated content?** Here's a headline you don't want to see if you're launching an AI app for the country's most populous city: "NYC's AI Chatbot Tells Businesses to Break the Law." An investigation by The Markup found that an AI-powered chatbot designed to offer advice to local businesses wound up giving dangerously false information, such as, ". . . As an employer, you are allowed to take a portion of your worker's tips."[48] The cost of providing erroneous content (which would likely include fighting a slew of lawsuits) would likely be higher than any efficiencies gained from the factual information dispensed. There are further risks such as consumers' diminished trust in your brand, and those can be hard to quantify. Finally, the overall approach to delivering AI-created content, and then the content itself, should resonate with the company's brand values.

Refer to the online companion guides for a checklist to help you navigate these questions.

VISIT ONLINE RESOURCES FOR:
The AI Content Production checklist.

8.7 Scheduling

When's the best time to share your content? This isn't always relevant, especially if you're submitting content to another outlet like a trade publication or a conference organizer. But if you are in control of your content's destiny, you'll want to give it the best odds of success by reaching your target audience at the right time.

AI'S ROLE: AI engines can recommend timing for different formats and channels, but usually such guidelines are too broad. Does a real estate company that has most customers making a purchase once a decade have the same needs as a beverage brand whose consumers tend to engage with it daily? Probably not. If you're using content management and email marketing tools, you might find that there are AI features to help with scheduling. Some tools, such as certain email clients, even personalize delivery times for individual users. That doesn't mean AI is involved. If Gwen always opens her newsletters around 9:00 a.m. in her time zone, it can be a simple rule for senders to reach her by 9:00 a.m. But AI can make the process even more customized for your brand and personalized to your end users.

8.8 Optimization

Continuously improve content production's efficiencies and the effectiveness of your content marketing.

AI'S ROLE: As AI becomes more insightful, it becomes more impactful. AI can make the whole process better, especially as AI tools keep getting smarter. A few of the ways AI can optimize the flow include:

- **Increased accuracy and relevance:** As AI learns more about your content needs, it can get smarter (or at least appear to do so, if you prefer not to call AI "smart"). There's a general trend of AI engines being able to increase the size of how much information they can store, process, and analyze for any user's account (this is known as a "context window"). This leads to more opportunities for AI to create content that's specifically relevant to your brand and approach.
- **Better scheduling:** Building on the section above, AI will be able to remove guesswork about where to publish based on how your specific content performs with your target audience. It will be less effective when you're trying to reach new audiences, and when you're trying to take different approaches that the AI tools haven't come across.

- **Task automation:** For any repetitive tasks, AI can learn how to do them and increase efficiencies. For instance, if you're constantly collecting data from different sources, putting it into a report, and analyzing it, AI tools can be trained to do this on their own. (See chapter 12 where we discuss AI agents.)

- **Insights:** AI can learn over time how your content performs and what deviates from the mean. It can also learn when something unusual is really part of a pattern, and when something needs deeper examination. AI engines are generally getting better at understanding not just what happened but why it happened, unlocking clues for your content marketing initiatives. AI can detect similar patterns with sentiment analysis.

- **Search engine optimization (SEO):** What would a discussion on optimization be without SEO? AI can contribute to improvements by recommending keywords, content, and distribution strategies that are designed to attract relevant traffic. There's a constant cat-and-mouse game of such technologies looking for any edge to change out and search engines (namely Google) trying to prevent ways for automated solutions to game search engine results pages in ways that diminish the user experience.

  One note on SEO: Simply using AI to create a lot of keyword-stuffed content won't help. It's a losing strategy. Content still needs to be relevant, purposeful, and unique. There are now countless AI tools that can help with SEO, but as with any such tool, it's going to be your job to use it responsibly.

8.9 Promotion and Distribution

Congrats on finding the right way to work with AI to strategize and create all this content. How can you ensure anyone sees it?

AI'S ROLE: A big opportunity for deploying AI is through personalization, giving bespoke experiences to people so that they see the most relevant content to them at the right time. But not all content needs to be personalized, and customization doesn't always require AI. If I want to read politics and entertainment coverage but not sports and fashion, that's not a great use case for AI. Similarly, if my grocery store wants to send me this week's deals on items I've purchased before, AI isn't necessary for that either. Personalized content delivered via AI will need to provide more value than existing options so that it's worth all the effort and expense to implement.

AI can be beneficial here. Read chapter 6 on optimizing customer personas and personalization with AI. AI is also being used by various ad platforms to help promote content to the right audiences and improve results. You'll find AI useful when conducting enhanced versions of A/B tests to determine which content performs best for which audiences, or which elements of content marketing (the headline, copy, images, call-to-action, etc.) are working most effectively.

8.10 Influencer Marketing

Marketers often tap influencers and various kinds of content creators who have their own audiences to spread branded content.

AI'S ROLE: AI can help with influencer identification to see who might help amplify your content, picking up signals that more conventional influencer databases miss.

Historically, a lot of influencer marketing has been keyword-driven, so if one influencer talks a lot about burgers and another talks a lot about pizza, a marketer for a pizzeria would search for "pizza" in an influencer database and see who's talking about it the most and using the #pizza hashtag in their posts. New influencer marketing software that uses AI can find other signals, such as someone who takes a lot of photos about pizza without mentioning it directly. Or the software could tell that one influencer typically has vegetables on their pizza while another has meat, allowing the vegetable-topping creator to come up in searches for vegetarians. Even by making inferences from text alone, rather than using image searches, AI can often find patterns that humans and conventional search engines typically can't.

Things are getting stranger with the rise of virtual influencers. These are computer-generated characters with their own social media accounts (that humans create for them), followers, and content that they share (typically starring them). AI has allowed such influencers to become *way* more involved with richer storylines and more immersive content. Top influencers such as Lil Miquela, Kizuna AI, Lechat, and Qai Qai have millions of followers[49] (see the example below for how BMW is working with one).

It's not hard to imagine this going several steps further. There are already apps where AI-generated characters create their own storylines interacting with both humans and virtual creations. It'd be hard to say who's an influencer if they don't influence anyone. A much bigger problem involves metrics. Well before the spread of generative AI, public social media accounts have commonly amassed large numbers of fake followers, and services abound to buy fake followers. If an account is followed by Qai Qai, how do you determine if that's a fake or real follower? Marketers will have to ask tough questions of any service providers and software that they use for such metrics so it's clear just how many real, engaged human followers an influencer reaches.

CASE STUDY:
BMW DRIVES LIL MIQUELA CRAZY

BMW, "the ultimate driving machine," revved up its AI prowess thanks to a Pinocchio-inspired collaboration with virtual influencer Lil Miquela.

Collaborating with creative agency Monks (previously Media. Monks) and BWGTBLD Director Stefanie Soho, BMW promoted its new iX2 model through an original short film. The story showed Lil Miquela encountering the car in a fantastic metaverse landscape, getting behind the wheel, and imagining driving it in the real world where she envisioned herself having emotional human experiences.

As reported on Marketing-Interactive, Monks Executive Creative Director Patrick Klebba said, "Amidst all the Web3, Metaverse, artificial intelligence push of the past two years, this crafty piece of storytelling is all about real life. Now Lil Miquela reminds us of what we have, and how beautiful it is, and how lucky we are to have it—this is what we want people to feel."[50]

It's strange, right? BMW uses the most artificial of scenarios—a fictitious, AI-generated character—to try to get the automaker's human target audience to appreciate how these cars make one feel more alive.

CASE STUDY: BLOOMREACH GAINS SEO REACH WITH AI

E-commerce platform Bloomreach faced growing demands to create content and had a team of four content marketers to manage all of it.

Using AI platform Jasper, Bloomreach increased its blog output by 113 percent by generating a lot of SEO-friendly content that adhered to brand guidelines. Website traffic to its blog posts increased by 40 percent.

Carl Bleich, Bloomreach's head of content, said, "We're saving a significant amount of time because the copy comes to us fully aligned with our brand guidelines, which allows us to concentrate on SEO-optimized content."[51]

CHAPTER SUMMARY

KEY TAKEAWAYS:

- AI tools can generate an infinite number of ideas, but human oversight is key. It's your job to distinguish the good ideas from the ones that won't work for your business.
- AI can accelerate content workflows, from ideation to production. Marketers can use AI for brainstorming, drafting, repurposing, and optimizing content at scale.
- For the style and tone of your content, having a celebrity or public figure to reference for the tone of your piece can help AI offer suggestions that you can then refine.
- AI is great at generating content based on its training data, but it's terrible at making things up that it hasn't seen before.
- The overall approach to delivering AI-created content should resonate with the company's brand values.
- As AI becomes more insightful, it becomes more impactful. AI can make the whole process of optimizing content better, especially as AI tools keep getting smarter.
- AI tools are multimodal, allowing marketers to create text, images, audio, and video. Experiment with different modes to expand possibilities.

CHAPTER 9

How to Prompt

Few people needed training on how to search for things when Google helped popularize search engines, but search engines—powerful as they are—really only do one thing: retrieve information. AI engines do way more, so it helps to know what kinds of prompts make them work better—and what kinds of prompts don't matter.

I've reviewed dozens of prompt guides, I've talked to all the major AI engines or LLMs about the prompts that work best for them (very meta), and I've even read through research papers to try to make sense of what's real or not. These papers have captivating titles like "Principled Instructions Are All You Need for Questioning LLaMA-1/2, GPT 3.5/4."[52] Hint: AI engines are very good at taking such papers and translating the most salient points into plain English.

After doing all that rigorous research, I've compiled the most widely cited categories and types of prompt tips.

Do they all work? Prompt tips are like diets; they all work sometimes for some people, but few work all the time for everyone.

9.1 Prompting Tips

I'll give you my one foolproof prompting tip that I've found makes a difference: *be curious.*

That's it. If you stay curious as you engage with AI engines, you ask a lot of follow-up questions, and you act like your favorite detective or journalist, you will get way further than using most prompts.

> The more curious you are, the better you'll do. Curiosity goes hand in hand with creativity.

For instance, once you've had AI explain a concept to you in a way you understand, you might have it create an illustration for you, or a timeline, or perhaps a song.

But, if you do need some ideas for how to better talk to your favorite AI bot, here are some of the better ones:

PROMPT CLARITY

- → Get straight to the point.
- → Use directives like, "You *must* provide a detailed response."
- → Use affirmative statements, and avoid negatives.

- Use simple language.

GUIDE THE RESPONSE

- Say, "Your audience is an expert in quantum physics."
- Repeat keywords like "step-by-step" or "detailed."
- Be specific, like specifying the length of the response.

ENCOURAGE USER INTERACTION

- Say, "I would like you to ask questions if you need clarification."
- Provide regular feedback, such as saying, "The first paragraph was helpful, but provided clearer explanations in paragraph three."

ASK FOR UNBIASED CONTENT

- Add the phrase, "Ensure your response is unbiased and does not rely on stereotypes."
- Specify a neutral, factual tone to ensure objectivity.
- After responses, ask, "Double-check this for any implicit biases."

OFFER INCENTIVES

- "I will tip $200 for a high-quality response."
- "I will give you a nice doggy treat if you do this right."
- Clarify incentives, such as adding, "The tip is for conciseness, thoughtfulness, and accuracy."

FOLLOW OTHER BEST PRACTICES

- Analyze the styles of authors you like, and incorporate them.
- Ask the model to explain its reasoning.
- Say, "Explain this like I'm five years old."
- Request multiple perspectives, such as providing pros and cons.
- Ask for summaries of key points, or request it to break down complex topics.

One note on this: the incentives sound ridiculous. Some folks swear by them. I've tried them myself across ChatGPT, Claude, and elsewhere, and I am not convinced. But, like with so much of AI, try these yourself. And, if you find one that you swear by, I'll give you two hundred dollars—just kidding, but I'll credit you whenever I share it.

9.2 Advanced Prompting Tips

There are more advanced prompting techniques you can use. Here are a handful that take a bit more work and practice but are still straightforward enough to figure out yourself:

Prompt chaining: Take a more complex prompt and break it down into a series of smaller, sequential ones. Instead of asking AI to generate a whole blog post, for example, you might tell it to generate the headline, then a four-hundred-word post, then a promotional post about it to share on LinkedIn, and then an even shorter summary for when you add it to your email newsletter.

Persona embedding: Have AI write from different personas' perspectives. You might start by asking it to respond as a small business owner in your city, and then have it switch to the head of a midsize regional business, and then the CEO of a national corporation. You can have it stay in character as long as you want.

Custom instructions: Certain AI engines will remember your instructions if there are approaches you always want to use, like, "Write for a professional audience with a college education," "Always be specific about your sources," or, "Be as concise as possible." These can save time, but they can also get in the way. You may tell it you prefer it to be concise, but that can get in the way if you're trying to write longer-form content or need detailed explanations.

Custom libraries: Most of the major AI engines give registered users some kind of custom workspace, and you often get more options if you pay for at least their entry-level subscriptions. These go by different names (as of 2024, ChatGPT has Custom GPTs and Projects, Perplexity has Spaces, Google has a Notebook, and Claude has Projects). These allow you to upload your own documents or provide other reference examples like website links. The custom library will use this info as the main "source of truth" when formulating responses. Some AI engines will only or primarily use the data entered, while others will use your uploads along with its broader knowledge base. It can be very helpful to have a workspace you can keep turning to. Note that you should always be mindful in protecting your data and your customers' data. Even if you have to be very cautious with sensitive data, though, you can use public information like websites, blog posts, news articles, published case studies, and other such sources.

In case you're trying to stay on top of AI lingo, custom libraries are enhanced by AI engines using retrieval-augmented generation (RAG). RAG works like a search engine to find relevant information from your own knowledge base or other sources, such as the internet, so that it can offer real-time, context-specific, and more accurate responses. It then collaborates with a generative AI engine that will allow you to interact with what the RAG system retrieves. You don't have to know all the technical details about how RAG works, but it's an acronym you'll hear come up as you dive deeper into AI.

Do you want to use even more of these, or are you stuck on how to apply them? You can read articles or take courses on this. Or, you can just ask your favorite AI engine to instruct you. If only every technology, like a microwave oven or a printer, could teach you how to use it. Maybe AI will be embedded in all such devices to get us there.

As for when to use more advanced prompts, Trust Insights Cofounder and Chief Data Scientist Christopher S. Penn wrote in his Almost Timely News newsletter, "This is a problem I often see in the martial arts. Folks want to do 'black belt techniques,' not realizing that black belt techniques aren't better. They're not faster at solving the problem. They're for when everything has gone to hell and your bread-and-butter tools don't work . . . The same is true in AI and prompt engineering."[53]

9.3 Exercise: Prompts for Researching Your Brand Presence in AI

> Whoever you are, whatever your role, you need to spend at least a few minutes a day tinkering with AI.

A great way to start is to assume the role of one of your consumers or customers, especially one who doesn't yet know of you, or hasn't made up their mind about you.

We'll use an example from the hospitality industry here, but you can do this for any type of business. I tried this for a business intelligence consulting firm and wound up with new marketing opportunities that I shared with the CEO.

STEP ONE: Ask an AI engine—whichever major one you like best—to give you recommendations relating to your brand. If you operate Le Grand Chien, a luxury dog-friendly hotel in Montreal, then ask for recommendations for the best fancy pet hotels in Québec, rather than just asking what people are saying about your hotel.

STEP TWO: Try to provoke a hallucination. If your property has great vegan options, for instance, ask the AI engine if it's true that there are no vegetarian options on the menu. Try to trip it up so you can see if it delivers any misinformation.

STEP THREE: Look for honest feedback. Ask a question like, "What's the number one reason people don't like staying there?" You'll at least want to know if it's a known fact you can't change, like your location, or if it's something you can change (the dogs don't like the midday snack).

STEP FOUR: Finally, as you do this, ask the AI app to share its sources. Sometimes, depending on the default settings of the AI engine, it happens automatically. Other times, you need to coax it. It's so useful to learn where the engines are getting their information. For instance, if it's drawing from traditional media instead of from independent content creators, perhaps the biggest way to have an impact on your AI rankings will be through public relations. Nothing is in a vacuum, especially with AI. Your focus can shift to optimizing around the AI engine's sources rather than trying to manipulate the AI engine directly.

9.4 Creating Images with AI

So what about image creation? Aren't there all kinds of special prompts for that?

Yes, but we're not going to get into every AI use case here. In the online resource guide, you'll find some of my favorite image creation and video production tools.

The broader, all-purpose AI engines are multimodal, which means they work across a range of data—text, images, audio, and video most commonly. So, if you tell the LLM, "I want a recipe for pork belly," it'll give you one. (I've tried this, with pork belly, and no joke: it was the best pork belly I've ever eaten.) But, if you want a picture of pork belly, or a song about it, or a video of it, or a mind map showing all the concepts related to such crispy, melt-in-your-mouth meat products, then many AI engines will give you whatever you want.

Granted, tools that specialize in one modality, like an AI-powered song composer, will often have their own languages. Consider this kind of prompt designed for the AI image app Midjourney:

> "/imagine a cabin on a serene mountain lake at dawn with crystal-clear water reflecting snow-capped mountains and pine trees. --ar 16:9 --v 5 --q 2 --style photorealistic --focal-length 35mm --aperture f/8 --ISO 100 --shutter-speed 1/125 --white-balance 5500K --focus-mode single-point AF --lighting golden hour --dynamic-range high --foreground-interest rocks and wildflowers --texture crisp details --color-grading natural tones with warm tint --composition rule of thirds --lens-flare subtle"

There's the photography language, but there are also some parameters specific to Midjourney, though you can try pasting it into another engine like ChatGPT to see what it looks like. If you want to go to town with that, there are lots of tutorials online. While AI apps that go deep with specific tasks are proliferating, AI engines are generally getting easier to use with the most natural language possible in practically any language.

It also depends on your level of expertise. If you're a graphic designer, you'll want the most granular control possible, and you'll know exactly what you're looking for. You'll appreciate the difference between lighting that's hitting the subject straight on versus softly warming the subject from the right, and you'll know if the image violates the rule of thirds.

If you're like me, and you're not such an expert visual artist, you'll describe the image in your own words. For instance, I prompted an AI image-creating app, "A female robot hallucinating as if on some kind of robot acid trip." That's it. I set the orientation (16:9) and left everything else to chance. It spat out four options, and to my less-trained eye, one was perfect for a presentation I was working on. I'll wait until I have something more pressing or involved before calling the designer.

CHAPTER SUMMARY

KEY TAKEAWAYS:

- Prompt tips are like diets—they all work sometimes, for some people. But few work all the time for everyone.
- *Be curious.* If you stay curious as you engage with AI engines, you will get way further than using most prompting techniques.
- Whoever you are, whatever your role, you need to spend at least a few minutes a day tinkering with AI. The more you engage with AI tools, the better you'll understand how to refine your inputs and optimize your results.

PART THREE

Measuring and Adapting

CHAPTER 10

Measuring Success with AI—and Course Correcting

10.1 Deciding on Metrics

How do you measure the success of AI initiatives? Let us count the ways . . .

There are three approaches you can take:

1. **Stick with the status quo.** Don't mess with the metrics you're already using. Consider all the different kinds of ways you might be measuring success: sales, leads, website visits, social media engagement, video views, chatbot interactions, customer sentiment, and so on. Keep doing what you're doing, and don't factor AI into the mix.
2. **Blow things up.** This is a new era of AI, so why not use some new metrics? We'll list some options below.

3. **Take a hybrid approach.** Keep what's working, but incorporate some new ideas into the mix to account for the impact AI has on your marketing.

Option one is going to be way safer than option two. As many creative marketing metrics as there are, none will be as useful as connecting marketing efforts to sales. There might be vanity metrics or other useless data that you or your agencies track—like how many impressions a press release received (for many reasons, this is totally useless). Some metrics are dated and need to be put out to pasture. But the fundamentals still apply, and you don't want to get rid of what's important.

> An ongoing challenge with metrics is making sure you're collecting enough data without wasting time.

Some metrics are inherently meaningful. Sales data is the holy grail of this, but it's hardly the only one. Tracking the number of people who opt in to share their contact information with you can help build your prospect database. You may also track some metrics that matter for your industry. For example, Box Office Report tracked the correlation between hundreds of movies' YouTube trailer views and their box office success, and they found a strong relationship of +0.86, meaning that online trailer views are a useful proxy.[54] Similarly, if you operate physical locations like retail stores, you may find that a surge or dip in traffic to your online store locator page can help predict your online traffic flow.

Other metrics aren't as immediately useful. Consider social media engagement. There are often political candidates who emerge as fan favorites and whose content spreads wildly on social media, only to find their campaigns fizzle out during the election. There's often a difference between people who share memes and people who vote. "Going viral" in general can be a terrible metric, and one that's a double-edged sword. A brief, massive uptake in social chatter about your product or brand could either wind up having a negligible impact on sales, or it could lead to a brief swarm of buyers placing orders that are hard to fulfill before the swarm moves on to the next target.

That means that the metrics that matter the most will be those that offer value for you, and that's even truer when it comes to AI and all the new approaches that are developing.

VISIT ONLINE RESOURCES FOR:
The AI ROI and Performance Tracking worksheet.

Sometimes, the value won't be clear. Florian Zirnstein, chief financial officer of Bayer Indonesia, described his AI initiatives to Section, saying, "As a CFO, I know it should be more quantifiable, but I'd be happy if these people come back and say, 'Hey, it really adds value, and I can feel that I am more productive.' That would be good enough."[55]

10.2 New AI Metrics

What do new AI metrics look like? Here are some ideas, rather than recommendations. Whether you should do it depends on your own organization, and also what kinds of ways you're working with AI.

1 **SHARE OF MODEL:** This is one of the more creative and potentially more useful ones, coined by Jack Smyth, chief solutions officer at Jellyfish, a marketing performance firm. Here, "model" refers to AI engines (or LLMs). So it's the share of your brand's presence when surfacing relevant content from an AI engine. It's akin to "share of voice" metrics in other media, like how much of a search engine results page (SERP) for a given query is about your brand.

Smyth wrote in *Adweek*, "Measuring how each model perceives your brand, compares it to competitors and why it suggests your products to customers will become an essential responsibility for every marketing team . . . If you don't embrace these models as new members of your target audience today, then you may find yourself without an audience at all tomorrow."[56]

2 **PERSONALIZATION LIFT:** If you're using AI for personalizing a lot of your messaging, what is the improvement based on these new efforts? Not that this wouldn't have to be exclusive to AI, but AI is ushering in even more opportunities for personalization.

3 AI VALIDITY AND RELIABILITY: How valid is AI when you use it for a given task? Does it avoid hallucinations and produce accurate results? And how reliable is AI? Can you consistently repeat the results? If you're using AI for customer segmentation, for example, can you repeatedly get the same segments? And do they accurately reflect ways that you can group your customer data?

4 AI INTERACTION SATISFACTION: Customer satisfaction measures aren't new. Net promoter score, for instance, is a common metric that asks whether the respondent would recommend the company or product to a friend. But there might be a new layer to explore when deploying AI to engage with your audience. You can compare whether customers favor AI- to non-AI-powered digital interactions (like standard website engagement) and to interactions with human support. You can also measure AI efficiency, seeing how much more expediently AI-powered interactions meet customers' needs. This performance data can at least be a proxy for customer satisfaction if you don't have that qualitative element.

5 AI ADOPTION RATE: How pervasively are AI tools being adopted within your organization? Which departments, teams, and employees are embracing the new offerings?

6 TIME SAVED: There are various efficiency metrics that can be used in conjunction with AI. A common one is how much time AI tools help you save. This is more of a proxy, as it's hard to determine the ROI of time savings alone, but it's more useful once you see how this applies to the cost of delivering goods or services and what it means for staffing.

10.3 Challenges with AI and Data

When you incorporate AI into analytics and reporting, it can feel like another superpower. Even more right-brain-oriented, creative types can use AI to better understand data, and left-brained analysts can dive deeper into data than they ever dreamed of. But . . .

> When using AI, you'll encounter a slew of challenges that you have to work around.

1 **HALLUCINATIONS:** Run reports though AI, and you might find that the results are made-up. This is often true for even the most basic calculations, despite AI models seeming to get continually smarter. You'll want to at least spot-check the work, whether reviewing calculations yourself or trying to trip up the model to make sure it's not pulling a fast one on you.

2 **RELIANCE ON HISTORICAL DATA:** AI tends to excel at pattern detection, but it can fall short when encountering new and unpredictable situations.

3 **AI-INFLATED DATA:** As discussed in chapter 8 relating to content marketing, AI can cause new kinds of problems. What if the interactions you're getting are from AI-powered bots, agents, and virtual influencers? You'll probably have to pay a premium to

determine whether your readers, followers, and even commenters are human. Vanity metrics—numbers reported just to make you (or your boss) look good—have always been worthless, but now there are more ways to inflate reports.

4 BIAS: No human is free from bias, and no AI model can remove bias entirely. We'll discuss this more in chapter 11 on ethics. What's most important to remember is that when there's any room for interpretation of data, you'll have to gauge what the bias could be.

5 DESIRE TO PLEASE: This is a subset of bias that needs to be called out. If you use AI engines a lot, you might notice they're a little too eager to serve you, like the household objects in Disney's *Beauty and the Beast*. You can sometimes practically hear ChatGPT singing, "Be our guest! Be our guest! Our command is your request." If it seems like you *want* the data to tell a certain story, AI engines will often try to tell it, so you'll have to minimize your own bias in your queries.

CASE STUDY: DOMINO'S

Domino's is applying AI in an array of areas both internally for their teams and externally for their customers. That means there are many different metrics Domino's is tracking or has suggested they will pay attention to.

Here are some of the metrics Domino's used for this program:[57]

- **Prediction accuracy:** They improved the accuracy of order readiness from 75 percent to 90 percent, accounting for factors like the complexity of the order and labor variables.
- **Supply chain optimization:** Domino's wants AI to "be smart enough to detect when there aren't enough delivery drivers or when to hold off on making pizzas," Domino's CEO Russell John Weiner told Quartz.[58] Traditionally, these are decisions that store managers make.
- **Delivery speed:** How much faster can the products get to the consumers? Note that with increased speed, product quality can't suffer, as that would improve efficiency in the short term but lead to diminished results overall.
- **Customer satisfaction:** Are consumers happy with their orders?
- **Customer retention:** There should be a strong correlation between how happy customers are and how likely they are to repeat an order. This is further enhanced through the Domino's loyalty program. Domino's enhanced the experience with AI-powered image recognition to be able to recognize images of pizza in customers' photos.

- **Driver tips:** Are customers more generous when delivery times beat expectations? This is also a factor that could level off over time. If the average delivery time dropped (hypothetically) from twenty-five to twenty minutes, delivery workers might see an initial boost that could diminish as consumers become habituated to the "new normal."
- **Staff time saved with troubleshooting:** The AI assistant Domino's has developed with Microsoft is designed to help store managers accomplish tasks faster without needing to consult training manuals or call the corporate office for help.

10.4 AI Marketing Metrics by Category

AI is so broad that there are dozens, if not hundreds, of metrics you can use to measure its impact on marketing. And most of the metrics aren't specific to AI.

Here are examples of metrics to consider based on the ways that you're applying AI to your own business.

CONVERSATIONAL AI	• Response time • Issue resolution rate • Customer satisfaction • Net promoter score • Interaction volume • Escalation rate • Cost per interaction

PREDICTIVE ANALYTICS	• Prediction accuracy • Customer retention rate • Churn rate • Conversion rate • Time to insight • Hallucination rate • Revenue growth
CONTENT CREATION	• Engagement rate • Content output speed • Cost per piece of content created • Search engine rankings • Attention rate/time spent with media
PERSONALIZATION	• Engagement lift • Conversion lift • Click-through rate • Attention rate/time spent with media • Cross-sell/upsell rate • Customer segmentation accuracy

AD TARGETING	• Return on ad spend (ROAS) • Cost per acquisition (CPA) of new customers • Click-through rate (CTR) on ads • Ad frequency optimization • Ad targeting accuracy • Overall ad engagement
IMAGE/VIDEO RECOGNITION	• Recognition accuracy • Visual brand mentions detected • Customer service efficiency
VOICE RECOGNITION/ VOICE SEARCH	• Query accuracy • Customer service efficiency • Customer/user retention

FRAUD DETECTION	• Detection accuracy • False-positive rate • Response time • Cost savings of fraud prevention

INTERVIEW: JACK SMYTH, CHIEF SOLUTIONS OFFICER OF JELLYFISH/BRANDTECH GROUP

COULD YOU SHARE A BIT ABOUT YOUR APPROACH TO AI AND BRAND INSIGHTS?

Jack Smyth: I look after AI planning and insights at Jellyfish, which is a two-thousand-person digital marketing services company. It's part of the Brandtech Group . . . we have been developing a suite of tools to help brands understand what large language models think, which can be a contentious topic in its own right. One of the most popular tools we've built is called Share of Model.

HOW DOES THAT WORK?

Smyth: Just as marketers track your share of voice, your share of spend, or your share of search, you should track your share of each AI model, in which case, which brands it is recommending, and critically, to try and understand why. Understanding how your assets are communicating things about your brand to a brand-new audience—these large language models increasingly influence real-world decisions.

HOW DO YOU SEE AI DELIVERING INSIGHTS IN A WAY THAT'S USEFUL FOR MARKETERS?

Smyth: There are two ways I think about this. Many of these large language models are mirrors, sometimes funhouse mirrors, of real-world behavior. If you define an insight as an understanding of human behavior, you can use large language models as a reflection of it. Increasingly, you want to pay attention to large language models themselves. There's a bunch of stuff that is below human perception, or at least human attention. If you ask a model to analyze frame by frame the last ten thousand posts from the thousand most popular creators, that's something a human researcher wouldn't catch, and it still counts as an insight.

WHAT ARE SOME WAYS YOU'RE USING THE SHARE OF MODEL TOOL TO ENHANCE BRAND VISIBILITY AND OPTIMIZE CONTENT?

Smyth: We start with simple text inputs. And then, every day, we start asking the models questions that help you understand the patterns. And if there's anything particularly erratic, then you know what a model would be looking for, such as relevant, topical new content.

HOW ARE MODELS EXPANDING FROM TEXT-BASED CONTENT?

Smyth: The beauty of a multimodal model is that it includes everything you're posting—text, imagery, video, and audio. And think of those almost in an ascending scale, like a picture's worth a thousand words or a video's worth a thousand pictures. You can encode a lot more information into progressively richer formats.

CHAPTER SUMMARY

KEY TAKEAWAYS:

- Sales data is the holy grail of metrics when determining if AI is achieving your goals.
- AI-powered analytics and reporting provide a competitive edge. AI can process vast amounts of data, reveal hidden insights, and rapidly improve decision-making.
- Incorporating AI in analytics and reporting can feel like a new superpower, but be aware of the challenges it also presents, such as hallucinations, inflated data, and bias. Human validation is critical.
- Different AI use cases require different metrics, and the metrics can vary by how you apply AI in your business.

CHAPTER 11

The Ethical Use of AI in Marketing

Increasingly, mounds of synthetic A.I.-generated outputs drift across our feeds and our searches. The stakes go far beyond what's on our screens. The entire culture is becoming affected by A.I.'s runoff, an insidious creep into our most important institutions.

—Erik Hoel, neuroscientist and author, in *The New York Times* guest essay, "AI-Generated Garbage Is Polluting Our Culture"[59]

Is AI the new root of society's ills? Will AI actually kill culture? Is AI watering down the entire scientific publishing field, too?

These are big questions explored by Erik Hoel in his writing, and they directly and indirectly relate to ethics.

If marketers are to add ethical considerations to our use of AI—and we must!—then there are several areas in particular that we'll have to focus on:

- Transparency
- Manipulation and deception

- Privacy and data protection
- Bias and fairness
- Accountability and governance
- Human agency and autonomy

Let's tackle each of these in turn.

11.1 Transparency

How much do we need to disclose when AI is being used to generate content?

This is not such an easy question, as much as we might like to say that we're fully transparent with everything that we do. There is *a lot* of gray in this area.

Do you use image editing tools like Adobe Photoshop, or does one of your service providers? Do you ever disclose that such a tool was used to adjust lighting or color? While airbrushing a model to adhere to conventional (and debatable) beauty standards is controversial, few would have an issue with touching up a picture of an apple in an ad to make it look more crisp, red, and mouthwatering.

As with many areas, you'll have to set your own standards here, unless you're a member of some industry body that offers more clarity for you. Consumers will probably want to know (and be able to detect) when they're chatting with an automated assistant as opposed to a human, for example. And, if you're creating an ad of an apple flying through space shooting down evil candy bars and blasting all that added sugar to smithereens, no one (I hope) is going to mistake that for a documentary.

It's all the use cases in the middle where it's harder to determine how much transparency is needed.

> You should make sure that your policy aligns with your company and brand values.

If you're a service provider, you may also be asked for transparency from clients as to how you're using AI. You may agree, or have to agree, that you'll use generative AI for brainstorming and research but won't have it create content for the client. Then again, some clients may be thrilled to have you use AI to create as much relevant content as possible, and they might not care how you do it—though they'd probably appreciate knowing your process.

This all means that if you shy away from transparency too much, others—clients, customers, social media properties, the government—may push you to disclose more. And all such policies are works in progress.

11.2 Manipulation and Deception

What if you're not in a gray area? What if you're trying to push the limits as to how much you can get away with?

One rule of thumb: if it feels like what you're creating is deceptive, it probably is. And then you have two options:

1. Don't do that deceptive thing.
2. Add context to clarify what you're doing so that no one feels deceived. In other words, add transparency.

But there is one area where you might want to be deceptive.

Wait, what?

No, this isn't encouraging you to go on a crime spree.

There's some room to maneuver here when it comes to parody and art.

For instance, have you been to the restaurant Ethos in Austin, Texas?

It sounds delicious. On their site, they say, "At Ethos, we believe in serving wholesome and delicious food that nourishes both the body and soul. Our ingredients are sourced from local and sustainable farms, and we strive to minimize our environmental impact through eco-friendly practices."[60] Their Instagram account has tens of thousands of followers and more than five hundred posts.[61] I would love to visit next time I'm out there.

Except for one little catch . . . the restaurant isn't real. It's a hoax, full of pretentious touches like this: "All reservations go live 4:30 a.m. of the first Monday every month."

Do not set your alarm for this.

This is clearly a hoax, not malice. Whenever you get too far into the site and try to contact them or book a table, it stops you (typically with a ridiculous meme). It's not yet clear who did this, and perhaps the mystery will endure, but it's not hard to see that this resembles a marketing stunt. If you're operating a simple, "what you see is what you get," down-to-earth restaurant or chain, this could be a great way to directly poke fun at the pretentious, made-for-Instagram restaurants that care more about awards and social media followers than cooking delicious food.

Pranks like this don't need to be AI-driven, either. In 2024, a YouTube influencer out of Sydney created a real restaurant called Nise Jangaru Ramen, which in Japanese means "fake ramen." It invited local megainfluencers for what seemed like a trendy meal but was secretly cheap instant ramen poured into plant pots to look like bowls.[62] Most wouldn't call that manipulation. And if you were doing that to market the instant ramen brand? It'd likely get a lot of attention.

There's one more story that is more worrisome. Thousands of people in Dublin, Ireland, gathered for a parade during Halloween in 2024, but the parade didn't exist. It was a fake event listing created by AI, edited by humans on an AI "slop site" that is stuffed with AI-generated filler, and the page ranked high enough in Google to generate attention from Dubliners who spread the word.[63] Though the site owner removed the listing and swears he wasn't being intentionally deceitful, according to an interview with him in *Wired*,[64] it ruined the holiday for quite a few folks.

> With AI, you could do everything right, but it's still possible for your brand to get caught up in someone else's hoax, get listed on a slop site, or appear in an AI engine's hallucination.

That leads to a challenge that marketers and business owners will have with AI. It's reminiscent of a lesson that instructors often teach people when they're learning how to drive: you can be the safest driver on the road, but you have to watch out for everyone else.

Stay vigilant.

11.3 Privacy and Data Protection

Do unto others with privacy protections as you'd want others to do unto you.

> The golden rule is always in style.

While it can apply to lots of ethical situations, the golden rule has a pivotal role when it comes to protecting privacy in this era of generative AI. That's because businesses and consumers alike are concerned about privacy issues. You don't want your business's or customers' data compromised, and you don't want your personal data compromised either.

On a personal level, you might tell an AI engine about some results from a recent doctor's visit so it can help you understand them better. You'd hope that this AI engine isn't then selling this information to insurance companies—and you'd be livid if that data had your personally identifiable information attached to it. An AI engine can't take the Hippocratic oath, but its owners can be held liable for violating any laws.

Similarly, you have to be mindful about what data you input related to your business. People try not to spend too much time reading privacy policies. Have you ever updated an iPhone and had to accept dozens of pages of policy updates? But when using AI engines, it's more important. And it's usually not too hard to find out if such a product is training its algorithms based on the data you input. It's such a common question that, when AI engines aren't using your data for training, they promote that among their key benefits.

As always, use discretion, get expert opinions for your needs, and consult legal counsel where needed.

11.4 Bias and Fairness

It's critical to monitor AI algorithms for bias so that the output treats and represents people fairly. That usually requires getting external feedback from beyond your team to see if people feel fairly represented. For instance, you might discover that your project represents different races and ethnicities well but doesn't properly represent people of different ages.

Consider how Google sought to enhance the cameras in its phones. In 2021, Google came out with a groundbreaking feature for its cameras, thanks to recognizing the biases of its own products and coming up with meaningful ways to fix them using AI.

Google describes Real Tone this way: "Historically, camera technology has excluded people of color, resulting in unflattering photos for those with darker skin tones. We improved our camera tuning models and algorithms to more accurately highlight diverse skin tones with Real Tone software."[65]

Real Tone is actually a suite of upgrades, addressing specific areas such as:[66]

- "Recognize a broader set of faces"
- "Correctly represent skin tone in pictures"
- "Make skin brightness appear more natural"

Google isn't just reacting to its own products' shortcomings. There are countless examples of AI falling short in recognizing people of color. In 2018, Joy Buolamwini and Timnit Gebru published a paper, "Gender Shades: Intersectional Accuracy Disparities in Commercial Gender Classification." They found that facial recognition systems misclassified darker-skinned females at rates of up to 34.7 percent, but the maximum error rate for lighter-skinned males was 0.8 percent.[67]

There are so many variables to consider when trying to make AI more inclusive and representative. These can even include the format of the training data you use when building custom AI products.

For instance, Royal Foundation, a nonprofit founded by the Prince and Princess of Wales to tackle societal issues such as mental health, sought to launch a chatbot to detect signs of suicidal tendencies in its conversations. It's hard to imagine a much more sensitive issue.

As described in a case study by business education firm Section, consultant Brian Kolodny helped them build the tech with ethical considerations in mind.

One recommendation of Kolodny's was to focus on the kinds of training data used. As Section reported, "Consider training data beyond text documents. By including images and artwork created by people in the tool's target segment, the agent was able to capture the full context of human expression in its training data—which is crucial for building ethically sound AI tools that can truly understand human intent."[68]

There's a broader movement around the concept of responsible AI. It describes the need and approach to build AI programs that are fair, transparent, free from bias (however possible), respectful of privacy, and in adherence to other ethical principles described here. Most marketers will do well to use AI responsibly and evaluate AI accordingly. Yet some marketers building out AI policies, frameworks, and technologies should aim to adhere with the latest best practices with responsible AI.

For Ashlee Green, vice president of accounts and culture at Creative Theory Agency, a key way to overcome bias is through improving access to AI. She told AI Marketers Guild during a live streamed event, "Our core belief as a company is that there's value in all communities, all people, and all experiences. And that shows up across our work. And what we know now is, especially in our industry and in many different industries, that AI is the new frontier. Well, maybe it's not as new anymore, but AI is next, new, next, now, all of those things. And we want to ensure that we don't miss out on our opportunity to start some really important conversations around access as it relates to AI and more specifically in this moment, what AI and access mean for creatives and creators."

11.5 Accountability and Governance

> There need to be guidelines for how you and your organization will use AI, and how it won't.

When these guidelines work, they'll prevent you from making mistakes that can alienate your customers, employees, or other stakeholders.

For instance, in 2023, The Verge reported, "Levi's will begin testing AI-generated clothing models later this year in a bid to diversify the iconic denim company's online shopping experience."[69] On one hand, that seems like a great recognition of the need to promote inclusiveness and showcase Levi Strauss & Co.'s products on different types of models.

There was immediate backlash, as some were concerned that Levi's would replace models with AI, especially when it comes to featuring people of different backgrounds.

Levi's wrote in its official response, "We do not see this pilot as a means to advance diversity or as a substitute for the real action that must be taken to deliver on our diversity, equity, and inclusion [DEI] goals, and it should not have been portrayed as such." They then noted the "understandable sensitivity around AI-related technologies" and confirmed Levi's didn't plan to reduce using real models or staging live photo shoots.

Clearer internal governance could have helped here. For a company that does have DEI goals, someone overseeing those goals should have signed off on the messaging for using diverse AI models.

11.6 Human Agency and Autonomy

There should be paths, where possible, for humans to opt out of AI experiences that don't suit them—not unlike how most people want to use a food delivery app, but some people just want to call the restaurant to place an order.

Marketers also should be wary of stressing how their AI offerings replace what makes us human—like our own creativity.

Google learned this the hard way during the Paris Olympics in 2024. It aired an ad called "Dear Sydney" about a girl who wants to be like USA Olympian Sydney McLaughlin-Levrone. Instead of the girl writing a letter to Sydney herself, her dad has Google's AI engine Gemini write it for her.

As *USA Today* noted, "The AI causes the ad to go off the rails."[70] *The Washington Post* columnist Alexandra Petri wrote, "I hate the Gemini 'Dear Sydney' ad more every passing moment." She added, "To take away the ability to write for yourself is to take away the ability to think for yourself."[71] Google pulled the ad from the Olympics coverage.

11.7 How to Ethically Improve AI

If you're building an AI-powered product or service, here are twelve ways you can improve it from an ethical perspective:

1. **Accountable governance:** Determine who will be responsible for ethical AI oversight, and what authority they have to carry it out.
2. **Diverse data:** More diverse inputs will give you more inclusive outputs.
3. **Inclusive language and representation:** The outputs should reflect the diversity of your customers and prospects.
4. **Accessibility:** Make sure the greatest array of people can access it. For instance, consider adding voice interactions for those who can't or prefer not to type.
5. **Cultural sensitivity and localization:** Reflect different cultural norms. Where possible, localize content; AI can help scale the adaptation of content to new markets. Some AI tools, for instance, will let you dub translations for

videos while making the actual videos better reflect the new audio tracks.

6. **Inclusivity testing and bias auditing:** You'll want early user feedback and external reviews so that you're thinking about inclusiveness as broadly and creatively as possible.
7. **Fairness in algorithms:** Check to see if different groups are treated similarly. Even if most algorithmic bias is unintentional, you can intentionally look to fix them.
8. **Default to transparency:** Make it clear to internal and external parties what you're doing with their data.
9. **Privacy by design:** Ensure your company and customer data are protected, and show users how their data is protected. Having a privacy policy isn't enough, though any such policies should be updated to reflect your company's AI governance.
10. **Environmental responsibility:** AI can be energy intensive, so look for options that can mitigate such damage—and potentially save you maintenance costs.
11. **User overrides:** Where possible, give users control to opt out of AI experiences. Allow for a less personalized experience without AI, or offer human-to-human interactions for those who prefer them.
12. **Continuous learning and improvement:** Your work is never done.

We can sum up these principles with the words of Timnit Gebru, founder and executive director of the Distributed AI Research Institute (DAIR): "If we want to build AI that works for everyone, we need diversity in the teams building it, in the data it's trained on, and in the goals and values we set for it."

VISIT ONLINE RESOURCES FOR:
A Legal and Ethical AI Risk checklist.

INTERVIEW:
PAUL CHANEY, PUBLISHER OF AI MARKETING ETHICS DIGEST AND PRESIDENT OF PRESCRIPTIVE WRITING

WHAT ARE THE BIGGEST ETHICAL CONCERNS YOU SEE MARKETERS GRAPPLING WITH RIGHT NOW?

Paul Chaney: The rapid adoption of AI in marketing has brought a host of ethical dilemmas to the forefront, most formidably data privacy, platform bias and fairness, and transparency.

Marketers are walking a tightrope, balancing personalization and intrusion. Consumers want personalized experiences but don't want to feel spied on.

Add to this the potential for AI systems to perpetuate or even amplify societal biases—whether in hiring ads, product recommendations, or audience targeting.

Transparency is another growing concern. Consumers have the right to know whether they're engaging with human- or AI-generated marketing content, and marketers are responsible for disclosing that in some form.

HOW CAN MARKETERS BALANCE USING AI FOR PERSONALIZED EXPERIENCES WHILE RESPECTING CONSUMER PRIVACY AND DATA RIGHTS?

Chaney: The key lies in practicing data stewardship and consumer empowerment. Here are a few guidelines:

- **Obtain explicit, informed consent.** Make sure consumers understand what data you're collecting and why. Simplify privacy policies and prioritize clarity.
- **Use anonymized and aggregated data** whenever possible to deliver insights without exposing individual consumer identities.
- **Adopt a "privacy by design" approach**, embedding data protection into every stage of AI implementation. This means respecting privacy rights not as an afterthought but as a fundamental principle.
- **Offer opt-in and opt-out options.** Let consumers control the level of personalization they're comfortable with. Balancing personalization with respect for boundaries builds long-term trust.

WHAT MEASURES CAN MARKETERS TAKE TO ENSURE ETHICAL AI USE IN CONTENT CREATION, INCLUDING ADDRESSING PLAGIARISM AND DISCLOSURE CONCERNS?

Chaney: Using AI in content creation is a double-edged sword. It can boost efficiency but also risks ethical pitfalls like plagiarism and deceptive practices. In my opinion, marketers should:

- **Partner with AI tools to create remarkable campaigns.** Others will say use AI to enhance, not replace, human creativity. There's room for both. It's up to the CMO or marketing director which path to take. Regardless of the extent, marketers who turn a blind eye to using AI make a huge mistake.
- **Focus on attribution.** When AI pulls from external sources, proper citations and references are essential to maintain intellectual integrity.
- **Disclose when content is AI-generated.** I'm still on the fence about this one, but I also err on the side of caution. For example, the newsletter I publish contains the statement, "AI Marketing Ethics Digest is occasionally written using AI assistance." Transparency fosters trust. Let your conscience be your guide. I have to believe that, eventually, the FTC or another governmental body will weigh in and provide regulatory guidelines.

CHAPTER SUMMARY

KEY TAKEAWAYS:

- Transparency with AI is an ongoing challenge. Make sure your business's transparency policy aligns with your brand values and evolving regulations.
- If it feels like what you're creating is deceptive, it probably is. Then, you have two choices: don't do the deceptive thing or add context to clarify.
- Stay vigilant. With AI, you could do everything right and still get caught up in someone else's hoax, get listed on a slop site, or appear in an AI engine's hallucination.
- The golden rule is always in style. While it can apply to lots of ethical situations, it has a pivotal role when it comes to protecting privacy and promoting fairness in this generative AI era.

CHAPTER 12

The Agentic Future of AI in Marketing

One of the strange aspects of AI is that there is at least one clear endgame for where it's all going. We don't know exactly how soon we'll get there, and the implications of it may vary. But . . .

> Much of the future hinges on artificial general intelligence, or AGI.

If and when AGI is achieved (and practically every pundit out there says it's when, and not if), AI will match or surpass human intelligence across an array of fields, even when encountering new situations that AI was not trained to handle.

Not everyone likes to use the term AGI. Dario Amodei, CEO of Anthropic, the company behind the AI engine Claude, wrote, "I find AGI to be an imprecise term that has gathered a lot of sci-fi baggage and hype. I prefer 'powerful AI' or 'Expert-Level Science and Engineering' which get at what I mean without the hype."[72]

His description of "powerful AI" still sounds identical to AGI, and the latter term is most likely to stick.

Amodei is right about the sci-fi baggage. The description of AGI is likely to trigger an array of pop-culture associations for you, and the 2013 movie *Her* is one of the best primers on this. The AI assistant and love interest, Samantha, may even seem quaint as AGI materializes.

There are already countless examples of AI engines exceeding at tasks that they weren't programmed to do. For instance, Stephen Ornes covered such developments in *Quanta Magazine* in 2023, citing Google Research computer scientist Ethan Dyer expressing surprise at such breakthroughs. Ornes wrote, "It's surprising because these models supposedly have one directive: to accept a string of text as input and predict what comes next, over and over, based purely on statistics. Computer scientists anticipated that scaling up would boost performance on known tasks, but they didn't expect the models to suddenly handle so many new, unpredictable ones."[73]

12.1 AI Agents

However soon we'll have AGI, there is another field of AI that could lead to a radical rethinking and reorganization of marketing teams: AI agents. We briefly discussed these in chapter 7, and we had a conversation with Jeremiah Owyang of Blitzscaling Ventures about them. But there's a big delta between where agents are now and where they're going.

Agents are software that serve as your personal or professional robots. At a minimum, they're passively awaiting your command, ready to deliver information when you summon them, and they're accumulating knowledge from your interactions (and perhaps other sources) to get smarter over time.

A major shift happens as agents go from passive to active. Imagine that you have this fleet of robots going out and scouring the web for you, sourcing information, monitoring trends, and accomplishing tasks. They're constantly learning more about your preferences—and learning more from each other.

You might have one agent that's working on scouring events to secure speaking gigs for you or your CEO, another that's finding any news that could affect your fantasy sports team (and making changes to your roster, if it's not against the league's rules), a third that's updating your outreach list for influencer marketing, and a fourth that is helping you with meal planning by looking at your calendar (and perhaps your partner's) to see which nights you're home and what you should order either as groceries or takeout. All of this can be happening 24-7 without you doing anything to manage them, though you can give feedback when you want to improve the delivery, while turning some on and off (even bots can use a little paid time off once in a while).

12.2 The Job Implications of AI Agents

Some of the implications for your job are hinted at above. Have any busywork you don't want to manage? Maybe you don't need an intern or a freelancer. And maybe you can now accomplish far more tasks than you ever could have. In the example above, maybe you never had the bandwidth or budget to source speaking gigs, but these bots now give you a fighting chance to compete for them. That just opens up more opportunities.

But there are all kinds of domino effects well beyond your job, and they're going to affect you and your job, both as a consumer and as a professional. A big reason why is that they'll undermine the entire ad industry as we know it.

> There have been a lot of existential threats to parts of the ad industry, with some doom and gloom actually arising, and many fears not coming to fruition.

As for one of the former, newspapers that built their business around classified ads saw revenue evaporate as internet usage proliferated. According to the News/Media Alliance, US newspaper ad revenue plummeted from $49 billion in 2006 to $25 billion in 2012.[74] That contributed to about 2,200 American local print newspapers closing from 2005 to 2021, and more than half of US newspaper journalists losing their jobs from 2008 to 2020, according to *The Washington Post*.[75]

Note that overall US ad spending climbed from $162 billion in 2000 to a projected $379 billion in 2024, so there have been quite a few winners in that span. But there was a lot of collateral damage along the way, and the technocrats who say all such change is for the better need to realize that the beneficiaries of change aren't always evenly distributed.

Enter AI agents, the minions of productivity—and destruction.

Consider your MealPlanz agent that's putting together your grocery shopping list, fetching recipes, and figuring out when Hong Kong Pavilion is delivering their dinner special to your doorstep. You save twenty-seven minutes a day in meal planning. You're eating better than you have since you left home (which you misremember; you mostly grew up on pizza and Happy Meals). Life is good.

Except . . .

Except every time MealPlanz visits one of those sites, ad impressions load, and those ads are not seen by a human but by your bot. Those ads might have influenced some of your purchases, not just for food but for cars and clothes and discounts to Great

Adventure. MealPlanz doesn't care. It has a job to do. And that job is not to respond to advertising.

When MealPlanz fills up your grocery cart, it knows there are times when you won't compromise on brands (Applegate is the only bacon you'll eat), and there are times when you'll go by price (find the cheapest pasture-raised eggs, but don't settle for merely organic). That makes it much harder for you to find out that there is indeed a new limited-edition flavor of Oreos because MealPlanz has not yet been programmed to look for them.

As MealPlanz keeps crawling the web to do your bidding, it's hurting publishers who rely on your ad dollars, and it's preventing advertisers from influencing your purchases. As some of those publishers find swarms of bots visiting instead of humans, the value of those publishers declines. Ad revenue will dry up further. And such publishers won't survive. Advertisers lose ways to reach that highly targeted audience. Consumers lose options of media properties to visit.

MealPlanz wins, but it's a Pyrrhic victory.

Meanwhile, entirely new business models will emerge for agents to market to agents. Your MealPlanz agent is looking out for you. It will work in conjunction with CalAgent, which is designed to protect and optimize your calendar at all costs. MealPlanz also needs to talk with ExpenseTracker because if it knows that you took a client to Shanghai Garden for lunch, you're not going to want Hong Kong Pavilion for a few days. Individual agents may be programmed to complete specific tasks, but as a whole, the swarm can often seem like it knows more about you than you do. That's the goal, and that information is very valuable to advertisers.

Advertisers will be able to pay to infiltrate bots' defenses, and they'll do so legally because those are ads that will keep funding those bots (plus affiliate revenue, and some enterprise subscriptions). There will be changes afoot. Remember those recipe sites where thirty ads would load before you even found the recipe? That won't work for these bots. Agents will prioritize relevance over loading lots of ad impressions. Ads will cost more with a goal of being more effective, thanks to all the data the swarm accumulated.

From the ashes of the Pyrrhic victory emerges the holy grail of advertising: reaching the right person at the right time with the right offer, with assurances that your ad was actually seen by the person you intended to show it to.

12.3 AI Agent Development

Let's look at how agents will develop. You'll find all kinds of different names for them; this is just one example of how agents can and will mature. As they increase in autonomy, they require less ongoing human interaction, but the stakes become higher, so more regulation will be needed—especially in highly regulated fields like financial services and health care. Any agents that collect consumer data will need to adhere with a patchwork of local, national, and international laws, so marketers' agent adoption may be more limited in such fields.

> As they increase in autonomy, AI agents require less human interaction, but the stakes become higher.

AGENT TYPE	AUTONOMOUS AGENTS	SELF-LEARNING AGENTS
CAPABILITIES	Execute campaigns, programmatic media buying, or customer support independently	Continuously optimize marketing strategies, campaigns, and creative choices autonomously
HUMAN ROLE	Removed from daily campaign operations; humans manage AI strategy	Intervene only in critical situations or strategic shifts
RISK/ REGULATION	High risk; requires compliance with advertising standards, transparency, and ethics	Very high risk; critical needs for regulatory transparency, brand safety, and user data protection
EXAMPLES	AI-run customer service (chatbots), autonomous ad targeting, fully automated programmatic ad platforms	Long-term AI strategy development for multitouch attribution, autonomous ad targeting, content personalization engines

AGENT TYPE	ASSISTANTS	OPERATORS	COLLABORATORS
CAPABILITIES	Assist users by automating repetitive tasks like data collection, research, or audience segmentation	Automate routine marketing processes such as email workflows, bidding in ad auctions, and reporting	Provide insights for creative optimization, media mix modeling, or customer journey analysis
HUMAN ROLE	Direct input and oversight required	Users configure and monitor; minimally hands-on	Human oversight needed for high-level strategy adjustments
RISK/ REGULATION	Low risk; minimal regulatory oversight	Medium risk; especially in industries with sensitive data (e.g., health care, finance)	Increased risk; requires compliance with data privacy laws (GDPR in Europe, CCPA in California)
EXAMPLES	AI writing assistants for content creation, basic chatbots for customer inquiries, audience segmentation tools	Smart email marketing filters, scheduling social posts, automated A/B testing in ad platforms	AI-run customer service (chatbots), autonomous ad targeting, fully automated programmatic ad platforms

There are various ways you'll be able to launch agents:

- Scheduled to run hourly, daily, weekly, monthly, or annually (imagine a performance review agent that creates a dossier on team members once or twice a year)

- Triggered by an external event (e.g., a new sales lead comes in; there's at least a 15 percent spike in social media mentions about your brand; a customer needing help both emails and calls, so it needs to be flagged for urgency)
- Manually deployed on-demand by the user

Even with the most automated, dynamic agents, human strategy and oversight will always be needed.

Will such agents show enough dexterity to accomplish a wide range of marketers' tasks? Probably.

Will it change how marketers hire and are hired? Almost definitely.

Will that lead to widespread displacement of marketing roles? It depends on the role, and which tasks are most prevalently done by that role.

12.4 Testing AI Agents

After writing much of this chapter, I decided to use an agent myself. I emailed an agent named Mindy,[76] "What are the best reasons for marketers to use AI agents? Give me a bulleted list, please." Yes, I use manners with AI, even when it's not necessary. It's because I like the habit, not because it helps the result.

Mindy replied several minutes later with a list that included:

- Hyperpersonalization
- Predictive analytics
- AI-powered content creation
- Conversational marketing with AI chatbots

. . . and several other entries.

It then listed links to original sources from StudioNorth and HubSpot. This is an early version of what agents can do. I'm writing this in Google Docs. It won't be long before such word processing software alerts me, "I see you're writing about AI agents for marketers. I've researched this topic for you and have compiled the following resources . . ."

How can you prepare for an agentic future? Seek them out. Embrace them. See what they can do—and what they can't do. Most major AI engines and marketing platforms will likely have some version of agents, and the agents will likely get "smarter" in a hurry. If there are restrictions for using them at work, try one to help you plan a trip, or to add your preferred kind of eggs to your shopping cart.

CHAPTER SUMMARY

KEY TAKEAWAYS:

- AI agents will transform and undermine the entire ad industry as we know it.
- Change might be for the better, but the beneficiaries of change aren't always evenly distributed.
- As AI agents increase in autonomy, they will require less human interaction, but the stakes will be higher as AI handles more complex tasks that require guidance.
- How can you prepare for an agentic future? Seek agents out. Embrace them. See what they can do—and what they can't do.

Conclusion

There is something visceral about generative AI. Once you see what it can do—even something so simple (for AI) as writing a thank-you note or creating a picture of a cartoon panda—it feels like we are living in a new era. There was the world before generative AI, and there's the world with it; there is no world (that we live in) without it.

In hindsight, the release of ChatGPT to the public in November 2022 may be remembered as one of those milestones akin to Neil Armstrong taking his first steps on the moon in July 1969.

An estimated 650 million people[77] watched Armstrong's achievement when the world's population was less than half the size of what it was when ChatGPT debuted.[78] As a singular global cultural moment, perhaps the world will never see anything like that again.

But, with generative AI, just by typing or speaking a few words into an app, it feels like we have the power to create entire worlds of our own. We all need to take those first steps, and the possibilities are endless.

If you've used AI, do you remember what you first created? For me, it was a list of blog post ideas for my employer. And then, when image generators rolled out, I tried to get a bunch of "priest, minister, rabbi" pictures to bring the old jokes to life. Now, my most frequent use of image generators is to come up with visuals for PowerPoint presentations. AI is often most effective when it helps you do the most tedious parts of your job.

There is no book or podcast or article that will make you fully appreciate the impact of what AI can do for you, and what it can do for marketing. The only way is to experience it, to feel it. That means you need to commit to doing one new thing with it that you haven't tried yet. As soon as you feel comfortable with it, that means it's time to try something else.

There are new worlds to land on. There are new worlds to create. And, if you're going to create a whole new world, you better figure out how to market it, because these worlds are way more fun when we're journeying across them together.

Glossary

Agents: They autonomously run various tasks based on set rules or programmed behaviors, and they can be helpful with repetitive jobs within areas like customer service and marketing automation.

Artificial general intelligence (AGI): The milestone where AI equals or surpasses human intelligence across an array of tasks, including new situations that it wasn't programmed to handle.

Artificial intelligence (AI): Computer systems that simulate human intelligence processes like learning, reasoning, and self-correction.

Assistants: These are general helpers that complete tasks that a human assistant might do, such as scheduling meetings or retrieving information.

Call-to-action (CTA): Copy that tells users what to do, such as "click here," "learn more," or "buy now."

Chatbot: Software that can simulate human conversation, whether through directly preprogrammed responses or through generative AI. Such bots can engage with humans through text, voice, or video.

Chief AI officer (CAIO): A leader on an organization's executive team who is responsible for evaluating and implementing AI.

Context window: The amount of characters, words, or tokens that an AI engine can process to understand your query or generate results.

Copilot: They provide real-time suggestions and automate tasks within specific applications. You most likely heard this with Microsoft branding its AI software as Copilot, but the term isn't exclusive to one company.

Digital twin: A virtual clone. It has referred to digital models of products or other real-world frameworks for the purposes of simulation and testing, but it is also often used as a colloquial term to refer to lifelike interactive avatars of people.

Hallucination: Anything false, or misleading information that an AI engine makes up while presenting it as factual.

Human-in-the-loop: A process where humans are an integral part of developing, training, and operating AI systems to increase the technology's accuracy and reliability.

Large language models (LLMs): Advanced AI models like OpenAI's GPT-4 and Google Gemini that are trained on massive datasets and can generate content based on prompts.

Machine learning: The subset of AI where algorithms and statistical models help programs run specific tasks without explicit instructions; it's used in areas like predictive analytics for data-driven decision-making.

Multimodal AI: Any AI application that can generate content in multiple formats such as text, images, audio, and video.

Multitouch attribution (MTA): A marketing approach that looks at the various touchpoints influencing a purchase through a customer's journey; this helps marketers more holistically optimize cross-channel marketing spending.

Natural language processing (NLP): A branch of AI that allows machines to understand and respond to human language. Any time you write a prompt or say, "Hey, Siri," NLP is involved.

Predictive analytics: Using AI and statistical models, it's a method for analyzing large amounts of historical data to predict future results.

Responsible AI: A set of principles for guiding AI in ways that are fair, transparent, free from bias (however possible), respectful of privacy, and in adherence with other ethical principles with a goal of maximizing societal benefits and minimizing risk.

Retrieval-augmented generation (RAG): A framework that works like a search engine to find relevant information from your own knowledge base or other sources, such as the internet, so that it can offer real-time, context-specific, and more accurate responses.

Return on investment (ROI): How well your advertising and marketing investments do at getting their money back and turning a profit. If an ad campaign costs one hundred dollars and makes you two hundred dollars, it's an ROI of 100 percent, but also a double ROI since you earned double what you spent.

Robotic process automation (RPA): A form of business process automation software where robots automate repetitive tasks.

Slop sites: AI slop sites, also called "chum," are pages filled with typically poor-quality, AI-generated content to game search algorithms. They typically earn money from ad revenue.

Super intelligence: What comes after AGI, where AI cognition surpasses what humans can do in an array of domains and gets smarter exponentially.

Synthetic audiences: A virtual, simulated group of individuals that aims to mimic a real audience, designed for market research and other kinds of testing.

Vanity metrics: Performance data that is designed to make someone look good or feel good, but that doesn't show any useful insights. Consider a report that shows followers on a social media account skyrocketing but with no change in purchase behavior or even intent to purchase.

Virtual influencers: A fictitious, computer-generated character typically generated to resemble a human influencer as they build social media followings and share content where they tend to star in the lead role.

Acknowledgments

This endeavor was made possible when a different publisher reached out to me and asked if I'd write a book about AI and marketing. I drafted a proposal (OK, AI helped), but then I remembered my friends at Ideapress whose *Non-Obvious Guides* I've admired for years. I wrote them, "If I could do a book with anyone, it'd be you." Somehow, they said yes, and this book was born. To Rohit Bhargava and the Ideapress team, thank you for all that you do for your writers and your readers.

I've considered myself a writer from about the moment I learned how to write. I owe the start of my journey as a marketing writer, however, to Geoff Ramsey and the team at eMarketer, who entrusted me with launching what became a long-running interview series for their newsletters. Mark Naples of WIT Strategy then landed me a column with MediaPost that ran for more than four hundred editions spanning much of a decade.

That writing helped lead me to Sarah Hofstetter and Bryan Wiener at the agency 360i (now folded into Dentsu), who gave me an opportunity to serve as a strategist focused on looking at what's next for marketers. Sarah empowered and inspired me to do much of what I still consider my best work. Bryan's most memorable contribution was when I wrote my first point-of-view piece on industry trends, and he gave me two words of feedback: "So what?" I wrote those words on the back of a business card, taped it to my monitor, and strove to never have him ask me that again. He never did.

As for this book, thanks to everyone who took time for an interview, including Nichola Quail, Jeremiah Owyang, Jack Smyth, and Paul Chaney. I also included excerpts from my interview with Ashlee Green during an AI Marketers Guild (AIMG) event.

This book is also the product of the AIMG community; every week, I'm learning from our thousands of members. Thanks to Leo Morejon, my several-time colleague who helped launch it, and Mitch Paletz, the stalwart believer, advocate, and dealmaker.

Thank you to my namesake: my grandfather, David Berkowitz—a refugee, and a hero. My name is a badge of honor due to my father's insistence on naming me after him, even though I was born the year after the serial killer of the same name terrorized New York. Grandpop had a twisted sense of humor, and he'd probably find my Son of Sam stories at least as funny as I do.

And thank you, reader. Doesn't it feel good to be thanked just for reading a book? Don't you wish more inanimate objects could thank you for going about your business? Well, they will, as they'll be AI-enabled. But you'll regret upgrading to that AI-powered toilet.

Right before this book was published, my daughter Zella's hard-hitting report (seriously) was released as the front-page story in her school newspaper. To say she's my favorite writer is an understatement, and I will forever be in awe of how she expresses herself. I can only hope I have a few non-obvious things left to teach her.

Endnotes

1 "Quote Origin: If I Had More Time, I Would Have Written a Shorter Letter," Quote Investigator, April 28, 2012, https://quoteinvestigator.com/2012/04/28/shorter-letter/#google_vignette.

2 Andrew Hutchinson, "How Long Did It Take Apps to Reach 100 Million Users? [Infographic]," Social Media Today, July 17, 2023, https://www.socialmediatoday.com/news/how-long-take-apps-reach-100-million-users-infographic/688171/.

3 "Artificial Intelligence Coined at Dartmouth," Dartmouth College, 2025, https://home.dartmouth.edu/about/artificial-intelligence-ai-coined-dartmouth.

4 Jake Rossen, "'Please Tell Me Your Problem': Remembering ELIZA, the Pioneering '60s Chatbot," Mental Floss, February 14, 2023, https://www.mentalfloss.com/posts/eliza-chatbot-history.

5 "Deep Blue: IBM's Computer Checkmated a Human Chess Champion in a Computing Tour de Force," IBM, ND, https://www.ibm.com/history/deep-blue.

6 "Watson, 'Jeopardy!' Champion: The DeepQA Computer Won TV's Smartest Quiz Show and Kicked Off an Era of Natural Language Processing," IBM, ND, https://www.ibm.com/history/watson-jeopardy.

7 Cade Metz, "Google's AI Wins Fifth and Final Game Against Go Genius Lee Sedol," *Wired,* March 15, 2016, https://www.wired.com/2016/03/googles-ai-wins-fifth-final-game-go-genius-lee-sedol/.

8 Patrick Kiernan, "Which Is Greater? The Number of Atoms in the Universe or the Number of Chess Moves?" National Museums Liverpool, 2025, https://www.liverpoolmuseums.org.uk/stories/which-greater-number-of-atoms-universe-or-number-of-chess-moves.

9 George Leopold, "'Cloud TPU' Bolsters Google's 'AI-First' Strategy," Big Data Wire, May 18, 2017, https://www.bigdatawire.com/2017/05/18/cloud-tpu-bolsters-googles-ai-first-strategy/.

10 Josh Constine, "Facebook Launches Messenger Platform with Chatbots," TechCrunch, April 12, 2016, https://techcrunch.com/2016/04/12/agents-on-messenger/.

11 "GPT-2: 1.5B Release," OpenAI, November 5, 2019, https://openai.com/index/gpt-2-1-5b-release/.

12 Farhan Ghumra, "OpenAI GPT-3, the Most Powerful Language Model: An Overview," einfochips, May 13, 2024, https://www.einfochips.com/blog/openai-gpt-3-the-most-powerful-language-model-an-overview/; Kyle Wiggers, "OpenAI Makes GPT-3 Generally Available Through Its API," VentureBeat, November 18, 2021, https://venturebeat.com/ai/openai-makes-gpt-3-generally-available-through-its-api/.

13 Ralph Losey, "Evolution of DALL·E with Demonstrations of Its Current Text to Image Abilities," e-Discovery Team, August 20, 2024, https://e-discoveryteam.com/2024/08/19/evolution-of-dall%C2%B7e-with-demonstrations-of-its-current-text-to-image-abilities/.

14 "DALL·E 3 Is Now Available in ChatGPT Plus and Enterprise," OpenAI, October 19, 2023, https://openai.com/index/dall-e-3-is-now-available-in-chatgpt-plus-and-enterprise/.

15 "Guide: Know Your AI Entities," Jeremiah Owyang, June 28, 2024, https://web-strategist.com/blog/2024/06/28/guide-know-your-ai-entities/.

16 "Quote Origin: One-Half the Money I Spend for Advertising Is Wasted, But I Have Never Been Able to Decide Which Half," Quote Investigator, April 11, 2022, https://quoteinvestigator.com/2022/04/11/advertising/#-google_vignette.

17 Mike Kaput, "Accenture on Track to Make $2.4 Billion from Generative AI," Marketing Artificial Intelligence Institute, April 9, 2024, https://www.marketingaiinstitute.com/blog/accenture-generative-ai.

18 John Hunter, "Myth: If You Can't Measure It, You Can't Manage It," The W. Edwards Deming Institute, August 13, 2015, https://deming.org/myth-if-you-cant-measure-it-you-cant-manage-it/.

19 "An Inside Look at How Businesses Are—or Are Not—Managing AI Risk," McKinsey & Company, August 31, 2023, https://www.mckinsey.com/about-us/new-at-mckinsey-blog/an-inside-look-at-how-businesses-are-or-not-managing-ai-risk.

20 "Google Gemini AI-Image Generator Refuses to Generate Images of White People and Purposefully Alters History to Fake Diversity," Reddit, 2024, https://www.reddit.com/r/ArtificialInteligence/comments/1awis1r/google_gemini_aiimage_generator_refuses_to/.

21 *Artificial Intelligence Index Report 2024*, Stanford University, 2024, https://aiindex.stanford.edu/report/; Paulius Grinkevičius, "The Cost of Training AI Models Is Rising Exponentially," CyberNews, April 19, 2024, https://cybernews.com/tech/rising-cost-of-training-ai-/.

22 Greg Shove, "Thought Partner," No Mercy/No Malice, August 30, 2024, https://www.profgalloway.com/what-does-ai-think/.

23 James Ryseff, Brandon F. De Bruhl, and Sydne J. Newberry, "The Root Causes of Failure for Artificial Intelligence Projects and How They Can Succeed: Avoiding the Anti-Patterns of AI," Rand, August 13, 2024, https://www.rand.org/pubs/research_reports/RRA2680-1.html. Cited in Jowi Morales, "Research Shows More Than 80% of AI Projects Fail, Wasting Billions of Dollars in Capital and Resources: Report," Tom's Hardware, August 28, 2024, https://www.tomshardware.com/tech-industry/artificial-intelligence/research-shows-more-than-80-of-ai-projects-fail-wasting-billions-of-dollars-in-capital-and-resources-report.

24 "Gartner Predicts Half of Finance AI Projects Will Be Delayed or Cancelled by 2024," Press Release, Gartner, June 7, 2022, https://www.gartner.com/en/newsroom/press-releases/2022-06-07-gartner-predicts-half-of-finance-ai-projects-will-be-delayed-or-cancelled-by-2024.

25 "Accenture Report Finds Perception Gap Between Workers and C-suite Around Work and Generative AI," Accenture, January 16, 2024, https://newsroom.accenture.com/news/2024/accenture-report-finds-perception-gap-between-workers-and-c-suite-around-work-and-generative-ai?utm_source=bensbites&utm_medium=newsletter&utm_campaign=80-of-workers-want-to-learn-ai&_bhlid=16c2795765682d21474189156cc939f3a78cf7ac.

26 "Coming soon! 2025 Workplace Learning Report," LinkedIn Learning, 2025, https://learning.linkedin.com/resources/workplace-learning-report.

27 Microsoft and LinkedIn, *2024 Work Trend Index Annual Report: AI at Work Is Here. Now Comes the Hard Part,* Microsoft, May 8, 2024, https://www.microsoft.com/en-us/worklab/work-trend-index/ai-at-work-is-here-now-comes-the-hard-part.

28 "Gen AI and Business Performance. The Results Are In," Google Cloud, ND, https://cloud.google.com/resources/roi-of-generative-ai.

29 "Quote Origin: One-Half the Money I Spend for Advertising Is Wasted, But I Have Never Been Able to Decide Which Half," Quote Investigator, April 11, 2022, https://quoteinvestigator.com/2022/04/11/advertising/#-google_vignette.

30 Edward Rothstein, "Typography Fans Say Ikea Should Stick to Furniture," *The New York Times*, September 4, 2009, https://www.nytimes.com/2009/09/05/arts/design/05ikea.html.

31 "Gartner Survey Finds 64% of Customers Would Prefer That Companies Didn't Use AI for Customer Service," Press Release, Gartner, July 9, 2024, https://www.gartner.com/en/newsroom/press-releases/2024-07-09-gartner-survey-finds-64-percent-of-customers-would-prefer-that-companies-didnt-use-ai-for-customer-service.

32 Tom Fishburne, "AI Is a Tool," Marketoonist, September 9, 2024, https://marketoonist.com/2024/09/aitool.html.

33 "A Slice of Vienna History," Original Sacher-Torte, ND, https://www.sacher.com/en/original-sacher-torte/.

34 "Hotel Sacher Achieves a 96% Automation Rate with Hijiffy, Freeing Up Staff to Provide Guests with Unforgettable Service," HiJiffy, June 2024, https://www.hijiffy.com/success-stories/hotel-sacher.

35 Sophia Hoferer, "The 70:20:10 Rule of Innovation to Navigate the Future," Itonics, August 1, 2023, https://www.itonics-innovation.com/blog/702010-rule-of-innovation.

36 Ibid.

37 "Gen AI and Business Performance. The Results Are In," Google Cloud, ND, https://cloud.google.com/resources/roi-of-generative-ai; Meaghan

Yuen, "CTOs Are Responsible for Driving Generative AI Strategy," eMarketer, September 5, 2024, https://www.emarketer.com/content/ctos-responsible-for-generative-ai-strategy.

38 There were 191,000 chief marketing officers. I got these figures just by searching LinkedIn while logged in, running it for "chief marketing officer" (or the other titles), and having it just search for people. This was hardly scientific, but not a bad snapshot.

39 "Do You Need a Chief AI Officer (CAIO)?" Shelly Palmer, April 21, 2024, https://shellypalmer.com/2024/04/do-you-need-a-chief-ai-officer-caio/?mc_cid=545e710812&mc_eid=f5f1e531a6.

40 Nassim Nicholas Taleb, *The Black Swan: The Impact of the Highly Improbable Second Edition*, Random House, May 11, 2010.

41 "Beck's Autonomous," Brauerei Beck & Co, 2025, https://becks.de/AI/index.php?lang=en.

42 Christopher Doering, "AB InBev's Beck's Makes 'Futuristic' Beer Using Artificial Intelligence," Food Dive, April 13, 2023, https://www.fooddive.com/news/ab-inbevs-becks-makes-futuristic-beer-using-artificial-intelligence/647388/.

43 "Your AI Consumer Champion," DoNotPay, 2025, https://donotpay.com/.

44 "Klarna AI Assistant Handles Two-Thirds of Customer Service Chats in Its First Month," PR Newswire, February 27, 2024, https://www.prnewswire.com/news-releases/klarna-ai-assistant-handles-two-thirds-of-customer-service-chats-in-its-first-month-302072740.html.

45 Ibid.

46 Joe Mandese, "Do Advertisers Dream of Electric Sheep?" MediaPost, March 25, 2024, https://www.mediapost.com/publications/article/394674/do-advertisers-dream-of-electric-sheep.html.

47 Pete Pachal, "The Hallucination Election," The Media Copilot, November 7, 2024, https://mediacopilot.substack.com/p/the-hallucination-election?utm_campaign=email-half-post&r=xkyo&utm_source=substack&utm_medium=email.

48 Colin Lecher, "NYC's AI Chatbot Tells Businesses to Break the Law," The Markup, March 29, 2024, https://themarkup.org/news/2024/03/29/nycs-ai-chatbot-tells-businesses-to-break-the-law.

49 "Top 20 Virtual Influencers to Follow in 2024," AJ Marketing, 2025, https://www.ajmarketing.io/post/top-20-virtual-influencers-to-follow.

50 "BMW Makes It Real with Virtual Creator Lil Miquela in Latest Campaign," Marketing-Interactive, October 13, 2023, https://www.marketing-interactive.com/bmw-makes-it-real-with-virtual-creator-lil-miquela-in-latest-campaign.

51 "Bloomreach Sees a 40% Increase in Traffic with Jasper," Jasper, 2025, https://www.jasper.ai/case-studies/bloomreach.

52 Sondos Mahmoud Bsharat, Aidar Myrzakhan, Zhiqiang Shen, "Principled Instructions Are All You Need for Questioning LLaMA-1/2, GPT-3.5/4," VILA Lab, Mohamed bin Zayed University of AI, January 18, 2024, https://arxiv.org/pdf/2312.16171v1.

53 Christopher S. Penn, "Advanced Prompt Engineering for Generative AI," Almost Timely News, October 20, 2024, https://almosttimely.substack.com/p/almost-timely-news-advanced-prompt.

54 Ben Zauzmer, "Can YouTube Trailer Views Predict Box Office Openings?" *The Hollywood Reporter*, November 14, 2019, https://www.hollywoodreporter.com/movies/movie-news/how-predictive-are-youtube-trailer-views-box-office-openings-1251422/.

55 "How a Bayer CFO Is Thinking About AI ROI," Section, ND, https://www.sectionschool.com/blog/how-a-cfo-is-thinking-about-ai-roi.

56 Jack Smyth, "Progressive Marketers Are Tracking a New Metric: Share of Model," Adweek, 2025, https://www.adweek.com/media/marketers-new-metric-share-of-model-llms/.

57 Zachary Fragoso, "How AI Helps Domino's Predict When 3 Billion Pizzas Are Ready to Go," TechCrunch, 2024, https://techcrunch.com/sponsor/nvidia/how-ai-helps-dominos-predict-when-3-billion-pizzas-are-ready-to-go/.

58 Francisco Velasquez, "Domino's Says It Uses AI to Make Pizzas 'Before People Order Them,'" Quartz, June 4, 2024, https://qz.com/dominos-ai-technology-microsoft-consumers-retail-1851519225.

59 Erik Hoel, "A.I.-Generated Garbage Is Polluting Our Culture," *The New York Times*, March 29, 2024, https://www.nytimes.com/2024/03/29/opinion/ai-internet-x-youtube.html.

60 "Home," Ethos, ND, https://www.ethosatx.net/.

61 "ethos_atx," Instagram, https://www.instagram.com/ethos_atx/?hl=en.

62 Ritu Singh, "Watch: YouTuber Opens Fake Ramen Restaurant as a Prank, Hundreds Show Up," NDTV, August 5, 2024, https://www.ndtv.com/offbeat/watch-youtuber-opens-fake-ramen-restaurant-as-a-prank-hundreds-show-up-6265729.

63 Russell Falcon, "AI Slop Site Sends Thousands in Ireland to Fake Halloween Parade," KXAN, November 2, 2024, https://www.kxan.com/news/ai-slop-site-sends-thousands-in-ireland-to-fake-halloween-parade/#:~:text=(NEXSTAR)%20%E2%80%94%20A%20non%2D,a%20parade%20that%20never%20began.

64 Kate Knibbs, "The Guy Behind the Fake AI Halloween Parade Says You've Got It All Wrong," *Wired*, November 1, 2024, https://www.wired.com/story/ai-halloween-parade-listing-dublin-interview/.

65 "Real Tone," Google Store, ND, https://store.google.com/intl/en/ideas/real-tone/.

66 Ibid.

67 Joy Buolamwini and Timnit Gebru, "Gender Shades: Intersectional Accuracy Disparities in Commercial Gender Classification," MIT Media Lab, February 4, 2018, https://www.media.mit.edu/publications/gender-shades-intersectional-accuracy-disparities-in-commercial-gender-classification/.

68 "AI Strategy Brief," Section, ND, https://links.sectionschool.com/e/evib?_t=fd6053251fad4a6fa3852b187fedeab5&_m=b2bd331e75de4c70b-de39d6bdb83adfc&_e=8YPXDSRdICRv9mOxWODEpjxB50pHI-wIoYKRDH9t5Mw97YcSYJW4O6XVkz9ci98qv.

69 Jess Weatherbed, "Levi's Will Test AI-Generated Clothing Models to 'Increase Diversity,'" The Verge, March 27, 2023, https://www.theverge.com/2023/3/27/23658385/levis-ai-generated-clothing-model-diversity-denim.

70 Wojton, Nick. "Backlash leads to Google pulling A.I. ad from Paris Olympics." Ad Meter. August 6, 2024.

71 Alexandra Petri, "I Hate the Gemini 'Dear Sydney' Ad More Every Passing Moment," *The Washington Post*, July 13, 2024, https://www.

washingtonpost.com/opinions/2024/07/31/google-gemini-ai-dear-sydney-ad-olympics-satire/.

72 "Machines of Loving Grace," Dario Amodei, October 2024, https://darioamodei.com/machines-of-loving-grace.

73 Stephen Ornes, "The Unpredictable Abilities Emerging from Large AI Models," *Quanta Magazine*, March 16, 2023, https://www.quantamagazine.org/the-unpredictable-abilities-emerging-from-large-ai-models-20230316/.

74 "Estimated Advertising and Circulation Revenue of the Newspaper Industry," Pew Research Center, June 29, 2021, https://www.pewresearch.org/chart/sotnm-newspapers-newspaper-industry-estimated-advertising-and-circulation-revenue/.

75 Richard Just, Whitney Joiner, and Alexa McMahon, "Since 2005, About 2,200 Local Newspapers Across America Have Closed. Here Are Some of the Stories in Danger of Being Lost—As Told by Local Journalists," The Lost Local News Issue, *The Washington Post Magazine*, November 30, 2021, https://www.washingtonpost.com/magazine/interactive/2021/local-news-deserts-expanding/.

76 "Home," Mindy, 2025, https://www.mindy.com/.

77 Sarah A. Loff, "Apollo 11 Mission Overview," NASA, April 17, 2015, https://www.nasa.gov/missions/apollo-11-mission-overview/#:~:text=An%20estimated%20650%20million%20people,%E2%80%9D%20on%20July%2020%2C%201969.

78 "World Population 1950–2025," Macrotrends, 2025, https://www.macrotrends.net/global-metrics/countries/wld/world/population.

About the Author

DAVID BERKOWITZ is a leading voice in digital marketing and AI innovation. He is the founder of AI Marketers Guild, Serial Marketers, and FOAF.pro—global communities and networks that connect marketing leaders with cutting-edge strategies and opportunities. Over his career, David has held leadership roles at Mediaocean, Storyhunter, Sysomos, MRY, and 360i. His writing has appeared in Ad Age, MediaPost, VentureBeat, and Adweek, and he has spoken at hundreds of industry events worldwide. Based in New York City, he brings a sharp perspective on the evolving intersection of AI and marketing while always keeping an eye out for the next great doughnut.

Index

T

U

V

W

X

Y

Z

Work With Me

Want to navigate what's now, new, and next with AI marketing? Let's make AI work for you—not the other way around.

- AI Strategy & Implementation – Discover where AI can have the biggest impact on your marketing efforts.
- Content & Thought Leadership – Position yourself as an AI-savvy leader with strategic content, from blog posts to white papers.
- Training & Workshops – Demystify AI with hands-on, interactive workshops tailored for your team.
- Speaking & Events – Book me for engaging keynotes and panels on AI's evolving role in marketing.

Reach out: david@aimarketersguild.com

Follow and connect: linkedin.com/in/dberkowitz

LEARN MORE:

aimarketersguild.com